Egbe History and Culture

James Dada
&
Titus Oshagbemi

Published 2008 by arima publishing

www.arimapublishing.com

ISBN 978 1 84549 320 6

© James Dada & Titus Oshagbemi 2008

All rights reserved

This book is copyright. Subject to statutory exception and to provisions of relevant collective licensing agreements, no part of this publication may be reproduced, stored in a retrieval system, or transmitted in any form or by any means, without the prior written permission of the author.

Printed and bound in the United Kingdom

Typeset in Arial 12/14

This book is sold subject to the conditions that it shall not, by way of trade or otherwise, be lent, re-sold, hired out, or otherwise circulated without the publisher's prior consent in any form of binding or cover other than that which it is published and without a similar condition including this condition being imposed on the subsequent purchaser.

Abramis is an imprint of arima publishing.

arima publishing
ASK House, Northgate Avenue
Bury St Edmunds, Suffolk IP32 6BB
t: (+44) 01284 700321

www.arimapublishing.com

Dedication

This book is dedicated to the souls of the departed founders of Egbe and the living architects of the town, who brought Egbe into the limelight, fastened the pace of its development and struggled to write authentic stories about the town. Despite the odds, distractions and difficulties which they encountered, the writings and speeches of the forefathers document the true history, culture and development processes of the town. We wish to also dedicate the second edition of this book to the memory of Solomon Olusegun Oshagbemi, 22nd February 1977 – 30th March 2008.

Acknowledgements

We wish to acknowledge, with thanks, the oral and written contributions made by each and every source referred to in this book. We are similarly grateful to all the sources consulted for their valuable suggestions and assistances in producing the book.

It is usual to identify the reviewers, Bayo Oshagbemi (Omo Awo) and retired Major Henry Ajetunmobi who edited the text and provided invaluable suggestions. We acknowledge the short notice within which Bayo Oshagbemi had to work and we thank him for his remarkable pleasantness, speed of operation and willingness to assist. We also thank Henry Ajetunmobi for writing the foreword and for his cooperation in arranging the photographs of some important landmarks at Egbe. The legal review of the book was undertaken by Francis Okwudiba; we are grateful for his recommendations. Portions of the book including Chapter 4 were specifically reviewed by the legal luminaries headed by Hon. Justice Fola Gbadeyan. We remain grateful for their advice and suggestions.

James Dada
Titus Oshagbemi

About the Authors

James Dada has an MA from the University of Kent, an Advanced Diploma in Educational Studies, MEd, and PhD from the University of Hull. He was a member of Egbe Town Council from 1960 and West Yagba Native Administration from 1962. He was Secretary of Egbe Development Committee for 18 years. His Titcombe College number was 12 (1951). He is currently a Governor of Temple School, Strood, Rochester, Kent and has an award in his name at the institution. He is an Education Consultant with Oxford University /Unwin UNESCO Project and was a Trustee of the Kent Refugee Support Group.

Titus Oshagbemi attended Titcombe College, Egbe, Government Secondary School, Ilorin, Ahmadu Bello University, Zaria, University of Lagos and University of Bradford Management Centre (UK). With a background in business administration and management, he has lectured at Ahmadu Bello University and at the University of Jos, both in Nigeria and at The Queen's University of Belfast, United Kingdom. A Professor of Management, he has written books on leadership, entrepreneurship and managerial time as well as several articles which have been published in journals of international repute. He is a trained management consultant and has wide management consultancy experiences in Nigeria and abroad.

Contents

List of Tables, Photographs and Exhibits	9
Foreword	11
Preface (First Edition)	13
Preface (Second Edition)	15

Chapter 1: Introduction — 17
- The Origin — 17
- The Founder — 19
- The Eleven Settlements — 21
- The Economy — 24

Chapter 2: Relationships with the environs — 39
- Origin of Yagba — 39
- Relationships with the Nupes — 41
- Protests and Mokobon Movement — 42
- Yagba Council — 44
- Rivalry among Yagba towns and villages — 45

Chapter 3: Common beliefs and practices — 47
- Beliefs and rituals — 47
- Initiation into womanhood — 51
- Age grouping system ('Are') — 53
- Traditional African religion — 56
- Other beliefs and practices — 58

Chapter 4: Chieftaincy institutions — 67
- History — 67
- Origin of Owa — 68
- Decline in the status of Owa — 74
- Chieftaincy discussions — 75
- Tommy Titcombe and Egbe politics — 78
- Egbe chiefs — 81
- Honorary chiefs — 89

Chapter 5: The legacy of the early missionaries — 95
- Early educational development — 95

The origin of Titcombe College	99
The principals of Titcombe College	102
Higher educational development	111
Egbe hospital – a major legacy	111
Christianity – another major legacy	114

Appendices

Appendix 1: Leslie's Analysis of Egbe Problems – Extracts (1976)	117
Appendix 2: Messages from Reverend Titcombe – 1966	119
Bibliography	121
Index	125

List of Tables, Photographs and Exhibits

Table 1: Early Settlers and their Component Settlements	24
Table 2: Egbe Age Group System ('Are')	55
Table 3: 'Are' Practices and Activities, 1830-2005	55
Table 4: Owas and the Ruling Houses	68
Table 5: Chieftaincy Institution in Egbe	70
Table 6: Traditional Titles, Origins and Functions	71
Table 7: The Rulers of Egbe (C1500 – 2006)	89
Table 8: Egbe Non-traditional Chiefs Appointed by the Elegbe of Egbe, Oba Denki	90

Photograph 1: Ajaforunti Sculpture (a symbol of peace)	Cover
Photograph 2: Pepelebe Hill (entering Egbe from Ilorin road)	25
Photograph 3: Egbe General Post Office	32
Photograph 4: Television Post (off Egbe-Kabba Road)	33
Photograph 5: Egbe Town Hall	33
Photograph 6: Oluwo, Oroke Ijalu taken from Ilorin/Kabba/Pategi junction	66
Photograph 7: Oluwo – Oroke Ijalu	66
Photograph 8: Old Official Oba's Palace (Ajewo)	93
Photograph 9: The Coronation of Elegbe of Egbe – Chief Olokundu	94
Photograph 10: Titcombe College	110
Photograph 11: Egbe Hospital	114

Exhibit 1: A Map of Egbe and Locations	34
Key to Exhibit 1: A Map of Egbe and Locations	35
Exhibit 2: A Map of West Yagba Local Government Area	37

Foreword

Much work has been done by earlier researchers into the history, culture and practices of Egbe and her people. But such works hardly did more than scratch the surface. At any rate, not much can be said for their incisiveness, expanse of scope and the impersonality and intellectual distance, without which a research work becomes largely pedestrian.

The present work by the joint authors is different. It combines a freshness of approach with delicate sensitivity in handling the materials and sources that turns the work into a collector's treasure. But that may not even be the book's best selling point. In its racy language and simple style of presentation, the work is most accessible to all classes of readers. Only those readers with a love for controversy can be guaranteed to find the work disappointing: the authors simply state the facts unclouded by sentiment, and allow the reader to draw his or her own conclusion without teleguidance or hectoring.

Yet one other strong virtue glows across the pages. The work is distinct in setting strict boundaries and faithfully keeping within them. Thus the authors are not over-ambitious. Rather, they are modest and honest enough to admit that there are vast areas still open for further research in the rich tapestry that Egbe history and culture has become.

I commend the book to all serious readers with a thirst for knowledge and truth.

H.A. AJETUNMOBI
(MAJ. Rtd) LAGOS, 2006

Preface to the First Edition

This book sets out to present the true history, culture and development of Egbe and to document the facts for posterity. This is especially important for the people of Egbe. It is our hope that the knowledge of the past will assist in some ways in steering future tasks appropriately and in initiating, directing and fastening the pace of economic progress, political maturity and unity in our motherland.

It is also our hope that this book will complement other books such as Simonyan's *Egbe Chronicle* (1991), Dowdell's *It Just Happens to Happen* (2002, 3rd edition) and de la Haye's *Tread Upon the Lion: The Story of Tommie Titcombe* (1995). We encourage other individuals to write detailed aspects of the rich historical, social, economic and political development of Egbe for its people and for her sons and daughters yet unborn. This is important while some older citizens of the town are still alive and can still vividly recollect the oral history, activities and traditions of Egbe. Indigenous scholars should assist not only in identifying various weaknesses and strengths of the town, and the behaviour of its people but also in proffering workable solutions that will serve to further develop Egbe.

We have tried to acknowledge all the sources of information contained in this book. We regret if any attributions are wrong or if we have inadvertently failed to acknowledge any sources used. This is especially so as some of the evidence obtained is from the oral traditions of Egbe as reported to us by various individuals mentioned throughout the text.

James Dada
Titus Oshagbemi

Preface to the Second Edition

Since the publication of the first edition of this book we have received several words of encouragement and support from Egbe indigenes and friends who desire to have the history and culture of the town in print. Some of them have also volunteered additional information for inclusion in the book. The following people read and made written and oral comments and suggestions about some portions of the book which we found useful in the preparation of the second edition: Diane Martin, Lyndis Dada and Tony Fagbemi. We have incorporated most of the suggestions received into the current edition and we would like to express our appreciation for their assistance. Whist Lyndis Dada proofread the manuscript and offered several suggestions only the authors are responsible for whatever imperfections remain in the book.

All the photographs are now properly headed and numbered for ease of reference especially by those people not familiar with the various items depicted in them. The book is provided with a name index which is compiled in detail. It is felt that the subject index which is not provided in as much detail can also be gathered from the detailed chapter contents and the list of tables, photographs and exhibits. The book is also provided with a map of Egbe and a map of West Yagba local government area, again, for ease of reference and study. We have added additional materials in several places throughout the chapters and we invite our readers to continue to enjoy the book.

James Dada
Titus Oshagbemi

Chapter 1: Introduction

Chapter One explains the origin of Egbe and suggests that there were people who settled at the site as far back as 3,000 BC. It narrates the story of Kelae, the founder who migrated to Egbe from the old Oyo Empire when his succession to the throne of Alafin of Oyo was usurped by his younger brother. The earliest eleven settlements in the town are presented before the exploration of the local economy of the town, at that time, was undertaken in general terms. In explaining the economy of the town issues such as its location, temperatures, soil type, traditional occupation and mining, to name a few, are examined.

The Origin

There is evidence that there were people who occupied the area now known as Egbe in about 3,000 BC (Crowder, 1973, p.17), during the Sangoan Age. This era was dominated by the use of stones and crude metal and iron implements. The implements were used mainly for hunting and grinding. Today, some people still do not have access to modern equipment such as machines for cutting trees, ploughs for cultivating land, mowers for weeding grass, etc and have to resort to the use of crude implements, such as hoes and cutlasses, for a variety of purposes.

There is a rock composed of a bow and an arrow carved out of a stone at Egbe. It is called *Ajaforunti*, a contracted word symbolising where Sango laid his bow and arrow to rest – after fighting and winning a protracted war against his enemies. Ajaforunti is in the Oluwo hills close to Ijalu settlement. Sango worshippers still have a soft spot for Egbe because of the religious and historical link with Sango. The Ajaforunti monument is a sculpture of the legendary Sango erected at the junction of the Ilorin-Kabba-Pategi Roads at Egbe. Refer to the photograph on the front cover of the book. Ajaforunti is a symbol of peace, strength and friendship. It was built by Jimoh Akolo in 1975. It should be clarified that Sango never fought against Egbe infantry but the place where he stopped all wars was at Egbe town. The actual place is shrouded in mystery in the

Oluwo hills. It is believed that hunters do not see it all the time as it appears only at random. Whenever someone wants to see it, the suggestion goes, it does not show up! It is therefore shrouded in mysticism which seems to legitimize its significance to its worshippers.

The legend about Sango suggests that the practice in the Old Oyo Kingdom was for the king to lead in the battles. Whenever there was victory it was heralded with songs and pageantry. When the battle was lost the king had to be decapitated. The fourth king of Old Oyo Kingdom was Sango and he was renowned for his skills especially in the meta-sciences. Oral historians suggest that when he spoke he spat fire and thunder. Therefore as a fear of reprisal from Sango the king was deified as incapable of death. His followers returning to the city of Oyo proclaimed that the king did not hang himself, 'Oba ko so'. Sango is deified as the god of lightning and thunder and worshipped widely in Nigeria, Ghana, Senegal, Cameroon, Sierra Leone, Jamaica, Trinidad, Cuba, Argentina, Haiti and Venezuela.

Other evidences of the Stone Age era in Egbe that were expressed in works of art have been confiscated and in many cases destroyed as the Biblical graven images were removed by the early missionaries. Such measures were typical of the iconoclastic era of the 8th and 9th centuries of Eastern Europe and the 17th century Puritans in England. Recent migration into Egbe was largely caused by what may be termed as push factors. Egbe, being an urban area, is surrounded by communities with poor standards of living, lack of good postal services, poor transport system and inadequate electricity and pipe borne water supplies. All these factors were aggravated by poor health services and the distance from urban based medical facilities. Many people could not provide sufficient crops to feed themselves and members of their families. Also, many people could not afford to send their children to schools. The educational institutions reflected inadequacies in the infrastructures and the available facilities. Many schools in the rural areas were built with mud bricks and have existed since the colonial era, which terminated in 1960 with Nigeria's independence. Yet, many of these schools have not been modernized.

In short, people migrated from the surrounding villages into Egbe looking for manual and miscellaneous jobs that they were best qualified to perform. These jobs were scarce. Usually it was the men that came first followed by their wives and other members of the extended family system. The main migrants were Fulani, Hausa, Nupe, Ibo and others from Yoruba and Yagba towns. Today, Egbe is a multicultural town composed of Nigerians and foreigners.

The Founder

The founder of Egbe was Kelae, a prince of the Old Oyo Kingdom who migrated to Egbe after he lost succession to the throne of Alafin of Oyo to his younger step brother. Kelae had gone to the farm in preparation for his installation. Prior to his arrival from the farm his step brother presented the insignia of office called 'adirifun' to the Oyo king makers. This account is similar to the biblical Jacob and Esau story in the book of Genesis. There was great upheaval by rival supporters. Kelae saw the successor as a usurper. In order to prevent bloodshed he abandoned the kingdom in search of a new settlement. He was persuaded in vain to return to his domain by the Owa of Ilesha who was his uncle. Kelae and the Owa of Ilesha had a bilateral agreement not to wage wars against one another and for Kelae to use the title Owa. The Owa of Ilesha thus gave him one of his own Crowns. Kelae later gave the title of Alafin, locally called Alaofin to his younger brother and put him in charge of all Egbeland.

The then situation in Oyo precipitated confusion and Law (1977) gave an historical account depicting a change of dynasty in Oyo in about C1500 to C1836. There were inconsistencies in reports by historians in explaining the changes of the Alafins. The chronological order of names of the Alafins was said to be put wrongly and in some cases four kings were said to have been completely omitted. It is believed that Kelae left Old Oyo in about C1500 but of this we are not so sure. However, Kenyo (1952), in his publication of the history of Yorubaland, confirmed that the people occupying the area now known as Egbe came directly from Old Oyo.

Kelae was both a farmer and a diviner although he was more of the latter. As a farmer he had his simple tools consisting of a hoe and a cutlass. As a diviner he had the Ifa Oracle and the family medical knowledge by which he was called 'Omo Awo', which means a child of the traditional medical doctor. Ifa Oracle is a set of cowries or kola nuts or shells of a tree tied together. The diviner usually throws this on to a leather sheet, a prepared sandy surface, or a calabash. This is followed by poetic verses and incantations with a trance-like performance. Kelae's Ifa Oracle had revealed that he was going to discover a new domain, a town where he would rule. The first place of settlement was Ijodo some 26 kilometers North West of Egbe. It extends from Iya Meta (three junctions) to Asiko land and Oro river. It was a commercial centre but dispersed by wars. The settlers fled to settle in places such as Egbe, Okoloke, Isanlu-Esa, Idofin, Awo, Isapa, Oro-Ago, Odo-Ere, Oke-Ere, Eruku, and several other places (Aworinde,1974).The then ruler of 'Oun' was just named 'Obaloun'. Oun is identified with the vernacular of the people.

When Kelae and his entourage migrated to Egbe they settled at Okoa and with them were their shrines and pantheons, all brought from Oyo. Some of the gods were Ogba, Obata (Obatala), and 'Are' which is celebrated by the age-group system. The link with Ijodo continued with rituals because of the abandoned shrines and pantheons. There are claims that there was always a mystic occurrence at both Okoa and Ijodo whenever a significant event was to occur such as when Owa Oguntosin was about to die at the age of 120 years. In 1968 a rainbow was said to have appeared from Okoa which landed at Ijodo location. It was believed that religious festivals with sounds of drums would have reechoed at Ijodo and that relics of dilapidated buildings and shrines are still physically visible today suggesting some truth in these historical activities.

It should be pointed out that, in addition to the original settlers or aboriginals, the people of Egbe include immigrants from Oyo, Ife and Nupe people who came to settle at Egbe in the 19th Century for a variety of purposes.

As indicated earlier, Kelae was more of a diviner than a farmer and the people of Egbe, indeed, the average Nigerian traditionalist, tends to be overwhelmed with divinity to such an extent that in every aspect of daily life the diviner is consulted. This has to have an effect on education. Farmers consult about the right time for planting and cropping as well as about the feasibility of some new initiatives desired. Bachelors may consult the Oracle on the appropriate girl to marry, a hunter may seek to know his prospects on a particular hunting expedition or an individual may simply consult the Ifa Oracle to find out his chances of succeeding in his proposed business venture. The whole community may seek divine advice. When Egbe was oppressed by wars, during the intertribal wars and slavery, for example, a diviner was consulted for advice. It was said that a hunchback man was needed as a sacrifice to save the community. The diviner, unfortunately, was a hunchback man! Not easily locating another hunch man, the community decided to use the diviner. But before he was sacrificed, he was said to have cursed the community. The curse was that Egbe will always be ungrateful to her benefactors by rewarding them with evil. It is believed that as a result of the sacrifice, Egbe was never overrun in the many internecine wars and during the Nupe invasions in particular. In a similar situation, Oshogbo town was founded for a peaceful settlement after the sacrifice of a set of beads to the gods.

The Eleven Settlements
The eleven settlements at Egbe were occupied by early settlers at different times. Ile-Egbe has always been recognised as the first place where the earliest settlers resided i.e. the first six Akus, namely: Okoa, Ijagan, Isaba, Ijalu, Otun and Odo-Owon. All settlements at the other side of Pepelebe hills, i.e. Ainke and others were referred to as later arrivals. These settlements include the five Akus, namely: Ainke itself, Ilemla, Ido-Egbe, Iloko and Opada, sometimes called Ipo.

Although the titles to the rulers of Ilemla, Ido-Egbe, Iloko and Opada have not been abolished they have been relegated to the background. This was because they were inferior to the Owa title system and the Akus had to submit to the authority of the

Owa title system on matters concerning Egbe as a whole (Owojaiye, mimeograph). Ododi is another recognised area of settlement at Ainke but it is a much later arrival and it is not therefore recognised as one of the original eleven Akus at Egbe. Ododi is also outside the city walls of Egbe. It should be pointed out that most of the time Ainke is used to refer merely to all settlements on the other side of the town which are later arrivals in comparison with all the Akus at Ile-Egbe. These Akus or sub-town settlements had distinct characteristics as is still reflected in their Oriki and Aku shrines (Owojaiye, mimeograph). See Table 1.

From 1920 the annual Egbe SIM/ECWA conference, initially called the annual Egbe SIM conference, started to meet at Ile-Egbe and later (in the same year) it would also be held at Oke-Egbe where the population of members was increasing. It was then that the terms Odo-Egbe and Oke-Egbe were widely used to refer to the venue of the meetings. Prior to this Ile-Egbe was used specifically to refer to the origin of the early settlers. At that time also Ile-Egbe and Odo-Egbe were used synonymously. The ECWA conference met (and still does) on the last Thursday of every January to discuss religious and evangelisation issues pertaining to all ECWA churches in the country. It is perhaps a tribute to ECWA that the religious meetings still take place today and the organisation uses it as one of the ways of managing the essentially religious activities of all ECWA churches in the whole of West Africa. They number their churches at Egbe as ECWA number one, two, three, four, five, six or whatever the appropriate number of ECWA churches built in the town happen to be. Today, there are more than a dozen ECWA churches at Egbe.

Historically, the then SIM church was built at the present site of Egbe town hall and it was simply called SIM church. However, it appeared that Tommy Titcombe wanted the location of the church to be nearer to him. In addition, as a result of the increasing population of settlers in the new development area at Oke-Egbe, it was decided that ECWA church number One should be located there. Therefore, the first church was moved to its present site. At a point, however, Ile-Egbe people complained that the location of ECWA church number One was too far away from worshippers and this gave rise to the building of the present ECWA church number Two at Ile-Egbe.

In effect it was the growth of Ile-Egbe that extends to and incorporates Oke-Egbe into one unified town called Egbe. It is believed that this was accomplished sometime before the turn of the 20th Century. For example, Egbe was long in existence before Tommy Titcombe arrived there in 1908. The unified Egbe was felt desirable for a faster rate of development in the area, following the knowledge that the population of a town was an important factor in the political calculation of needed amenities and subventions, etc.

As an example of later settlements, most of the land now occupied by Okedisin, Ogbonimosi, Ododi, Iloko, Egbe Hospital and Titcombe College are owned by Ijagan people (Aworo, 1982, 2003). Below is a Table showing the early settlers and their component settlements. In the late 19th Century, these areas were well delineated and functioning well. For example, the diaries of Lord Lugard were reported to have contained accounts that he passed through Lawiri and Ofili rivers and that he stopped at Egbe to purchase food to continue his journey. He was also reported to have described Egbe as a 'large town' where the people had stories to tell and where he was nicknamed 'Oyinbo Okuru' – 'the White man at Okuru'. Okuru is a land where Lord Lugard camped.

Table 1: Early Settlers and their Component Settlements

	Akus	Origin
1	Okoa	The first settlers to arrive. It is the oldest of all Akus. Okoa is therefore the cradle of Egbe. When there was a decision on who to be made Owa, the head had the last say. In battles, Okoa led the infantry and was renowned for their superior intelligence and military tactics.
2	Ijagan	The second set of settlers to arrive, next to Okoa in seniority. They own the present areas of Okedisin, Ogbonimosi, Ododi, Titcombe College, Egbe Hospital, Iloko, Egbe Girls College, Egbe Town Hall and part of Pepelebe.
3	Isaba	There are two stories explaining the origin of these settlers. (1) The settlers of Isaba left Okoa after a dispute in a compound called 'ile elejo' for Okoroko compound in Isaba today. (2) Masaba, an Etsu of Nupe from Bida made it a place of refuge – "isaba".
4	Ijalu	Settlers were from Oke Agun, Obele, Agbara Osin near Oro river.
5	Otun	Settlers were from Ijodo partner to Okoa. They own the Amokele area, the present site of the Comprehensive School and part of Pepelebe.
6	Odo-Owon	Settlers were from near the river Kasan, Oribo adetutu near Oro river.
7	Ainke (Ahinke) (Ayin Oke)	It means at the rear side of the hills. Ainke is composed of three brothers who later followed Kelae from old Oyo. Kelae gave one brother the land at the upper side of 'akin' tree, by which the settlement is called Okedisin, 'Oke idi isin'. The second brother was given Ogba 'Onimosi' a garden owned by a gardener called 'Onimosi'. The third brother was given an area identified by the muddy and clay land, 'ibi potopoto' from which we get 'Apoto'. (Toba Awarun, 1974)
8	Ilemla	Settlers came from Bida and their chief is called 'Emla'. Their ruler is called Emla.
9	Ido-Egbe	The origin of this group of settlers is being investigated. Their ruler is called Odofin.
10	Iloko	The origin of this group of settlers is being investigated. They lived outside the city walls and their ruler is called Oba L'oko.
11	Opada (Ipo)	Settlers came from Igbo-Oloro, the western side of their present occupation. Their chief is called Oba Opada.

The Economy

Egbe is a town in Kogi State, Nigeria, which has its headquarters at Lokoja. It is located to the east of Kwara State with its own headquarters at Ilorin. According to the 1990 Nigerian population census, Egbe had about fifty thousand inhabitants but the projected population today is well over sixty thousand. Indeed, according to the 2006 Nigerian population census figures, Egbe had a population of 73,217 while the total population for the whole of West Yagba local government area was 140,150. This leaves the Area Council (Akumejo) with a total population of 66,953. As Egbe has over 52 percent of the overall population of West Yagba, it is clearly the most populous and modern town in the local government area.

Photograph 2 shows the entrance to the town taken from Pepelebe Hill on Ilorin Road. The town lies approximately midway between Ilorin and the river Niger in the North Eastern part of the middlebelt part of Nigeria. It is approximately 100 square kilometres in area of land. It is a melting pot and meeting point of roads from Pategi (about 79 kilometres away), Ilorin (137), Kabba (79), Oke-Ere (4), Koro (8), and Odo-Ere (3). Egbe is surrounded by seven hills which form a sort of fortress or defence – Tanloko, Kelae, Adiro, Pepelebe, Ogo, Oluwo and Ogele. These wooded hills are analogous to the seven hills surrounding Jerusalem and this feature has made many people including the early missionaries to refer to Egbe as a Jerusalem in Nigeria, a haven for the oppressed, the homeless, refugees and slaves.

Photograph 2: Pepelebe Hill (entering Egbe from Ilorin road)

Located in the grassland region of Nigeria, Egbe's physical features contain inselberg on the outskirts and these hard granite rocks are valued for building and construction purposes. Two main types of soil can be identified at Egbe and environs. One, it has loose sandy soil mixed with dead organic matters and this provides pockets of fertile farmlands at the feet and on the slopes of the hills. This type of soil, called alluvial soil, also exists in the very many river belts in and around the town. Alluvial soil is reputed for growing vegetables and early yams which are valued by the inhabitants. Two, there is the type of sandy soil which results from leaching due to the alternating wet and dry seasons of the climate. This type of soil presents erosion problems throughout the town especially during the heavy rainy periods. Drainage is therefore a difficult and endemic problem in the town.

Temperatures at Egbe, like in other parts of Nigeria, are generally high; diurnal variations being more pronounced than seasonal ones. The highest temperatures occur during the dry season. The average highs and lows for Egbe are estimated to be about $32°$ C and $21°$ C in January and $28 °$ C and $22 °$ C in June. The average temperatures therefore tend to vary very little throughout the year. The rainfall averages no less than 50 inches in any year. The rainy season starts about late March and continues until about September. The harmattan period runs from about November until February and during this period the wind blows cold air from the northeast desert. The weather warms up from February to April when we have the hottest period during the year. Topographically the town stands at about 320 metres above sea level. All over and around the town are tall bean trees and palm trees which stand out against the skyline and which are often utilised by some of the traders in various ways. For example, palm trees are useful for producing palm oil, palm kernels and palm wine which are enjoyed by the inhabitants.

Historically and to a large extent up to the present time, the people of Egbe are predominantly farmers and artisans. Agriculture is a mainstay and the farmers make great use of the river courses around the town to grow a variety of vegetables in the dry season. The main food crops include yam, cassava, guinea corn, rice, millet, beans, sweet potato, tobacco and cotton. Cottage industries, such as earth-ware pot making and weaving, used to flourish but these appear to be decreasing in scale and importance today. This is due to the modernisation of the production processes involved in making these basic amenities and the resulting cheap prices at which alternative and possibly better products can be purchased.

In the mid 1970s to the mid 1980s, Phillip Morris (Nigeria) Limited promoted the production of substantial quantities of commercial tobacco around the town although the company has since folded up. Some petty and large scale traders, hoteliers, motor, radio and auto cycle mechanics and various other grades of artisans operate their enterprises in and around the town. One can observe traces of the colonial mentality syndromes being exhibited by some of these artisans. For example you may still find the sign board of some roadside mechanics reading Dr of mechanics or some artisans calling themselves Dr of wood or Dr of shoes. As in all societies there are, of course, other categories of jobs at Egbe. These are found in educational, medical and governmental institutions.

Mining in Egbe and environs was at its peak during the years 1926 to 1960, especially during and after the Second World War. The miner's office was located at Ogele hill. Egbe, Omi, Oke-Ere and Odo-Ere are noted for large deposits of columbite, tantalite and iron ore. Mr Hamber, a London born engineer, was reported to have made a fortune from his business dealing with the sale of these metals. Mr Hamber was reported to have got married and returned to London where he died but his body was cremated and returned to Okutadudu, Odo-Ere, where he erected his building. Another engineer, Mr Paravacin, was reported to have returned to settle finally in London after making big sums of money from his mining business at Egbe.

Electricity was initially provided by the Federal Rural Electricity Board which had its main office in Egbe for the West Yagba and part of Ekiti Districts of Kwara State. It is now supplied by the National Electricity Power Authority (NEPA) or known by its current name, Power Holding Company of Nigeria (PHCN). The pipe borne water supply was supported by the community effort and a missionary from Canada, Mr Bartlett.

There was a local cinema theatre, an air-field able to land small airplanes, Egbe hospital with a Nurses and Midwifery Training Institute, a number of private clinics, medicine stores, Titcombe College, Egbe Girls College, Egbe Comprehensive College, George Campion Academy, Government Secondary School and several nursery and primary schools. The infrastructural provisions were therefore not terribly inadequate, at least, by the standard of yesteryears.

The local economy comprised private entrepreneurs who normally operate on a small scale basis, employing school leavers, their own children and paid labourers in the pursuit of their activities. Femi Kayode wrote that since a long time, Egbe has served as an important market centre for traders of Yagba as well as those from Ebira, Abunnu, Oranre and other towns in Kogi, Ekiti and Kwara States. Long distance traders from Bida stop over at Egbe en route to such far away places as Lagos and Calabar in the south and Kano in the north. It is because of its strategic location that Egbe was felt to be conveniently positioned for economic importance and to become an early candidate for industrial development (Kayode, 2003, p.4-5).

Kayode highlighted three economic growth factors favouring Egbe to include (1) the development of Abuja and the consequent reconstruction and rehabilitation of the Abuja-Egbe-Lagos road that make Egbe a convenient midway part between Lagos and Abuja; (2) the availability of more reliable information on the mineral resources of Egbe and its environ; (3) the development of the Omi dam with a complex of down stream irrigation channels which offers immense investment opportunities for all categories of entrepreneurs. The report of a study commissioned in 1975 by the Kwara State Government stated that Egbe is a thriving Yoruba town and that it is one of the larger towns on the Ilorin-Lokoja road.

Writing about some agricultural and industrial potentials of Egbe, Igunnu (1993) stated that Egbe is a town which is endowed with much agricultural and industrial potential. The topography and soils of Egbe are very fertile and could be developed into productive farms both for crops and livestock. The 'rolling meadows' which are largely abundant are suitable for large scale agricultural mechanisation. Our fore-fathers, through their wisdom and understanding of the changing pattern of the weather, have mastered to a large extent the suitable periods when to till their farms and plant their assorted crops in order to obtain very high yields and profits.

Among the assortments of food crops being produced by the great Egbe farmers are yams, 'Isu'. Early yams are produced in 'Fadama' swampy lands (Akuro or Okete) while late yams or upland yams 'Isu Ote' are grown in abundance in Egbe. Some varieties of early yams from 'Akuro' do mature for harvesting as early as May or June every year, while the bulk of the yams produced are ready for harvesting from the month of August every year.

According to Igunnu, traditionally most indigenes of Egbe love to eat pounded yam (iyan) with bean soup (alapa). It is suggested that this is one of the reasons why during traditional wedding in Egbe loads of yams are demanded by parents-in-laws from the bridegroom. Indigenous sons and daughters as well as visitors enjoy various nourishing dishes made from yams by Egbe people. Cassava (Paki, Ege, or Rogó) is another major staple crop which Egbe farmers are noted for. As we all know, Cassava is useful both for industrial purposes in addition to being a staple food in form of gari, eba, fufu, lafun starch, etc. Egbe people and visitors develop tastes for a wide variety of the local dishes and delicacies.

The tender terminal buds of the cassava plant are used by the energetic Egbe farmers as vegetable soups. It can be so satisfying and nourishing to feed on such soups which are often cooked in the farmsteads with plenty of bush meat such as grass cutters, (Eku/Oya) giant bush rats (Okete), big frogs (alakata) assorted fish, deer (Agbonrin/Igala) and different types of reptiles, python (Ojola), crocodiles (Oni), etc.

Continuing his information, Igunnu also said that in Egbe, cereal crops such as maize (agbado), guinea corn (oka baba), millet (emeye/jero) and rice (iresi), are being produced to feed her teeming population all the year round. It is interesting to note that there are some traditional ceremonies which are performed to herald the commencement or harvesting of the planting season. For example, the 'Igbemo Festival' usually coincides with the appropriate time to plant guinea corn while the celebration of 'Epa Festival' marks the official commencement of the eating of new yams. These ceremonies are performed every year.

From ancient times the Egbe people have been great traders and economists. The people firmly belief that it is important to produce cash crops to earn revenue for the development of their town. Among the cash crops of Egbe farmers are Tobacco (Taba) which brought many tobacco traders from Ijesa, Osogbo and Ijebuland into Egbe. These traders specialise in buying high grade tobacco which they in turn sell to cigarette manufacturers at Ibadan and overseas.

Whenever yams, cassava, maize, oranges and vegetables are in season very lucrative trades are transacted at Egbe market (Oja Egbe). Thus a symbolic cultural effect of trading in farm products often led to intertribal marriages. This is very true in the case of Egbe people, the Ijesas, the Nupes and other ethnic groups around Egbeland. The historians, therefore, would be delighted to substantiate the roots of the assorted surnames and 'orikis' found in Egbe today. Perhaps they are related to these intertribal marriages.

Among some of the economic trees found in Egbe town are the locust bean tree (igba/iyere) from which iru famous for making soup are made. 'Iru' is a product similar to maggi or knorr cubes currently used for adding or improving taste to a variety of dishes when cooking. There are many palm trees from which palm-wine tappers bring down 'palmy' every day for recouping the energies of the farmers after the hard days labour. The palm trees also produce palm oil and palm kernel oil for various domestic and industrial uses such as soap detergents and pomades (adin). Egbe town in the olden days had many baobab trees (igi ose) which our grand-parents (researchers/inventors) were processing into local salt (obu) even before the arrival of the present table salt. These traditional and salt industries should not be allowed to die in an age obsessed with Western discoveries. The medicinal and curative potentials of the indigenous products must be explored.

Indeed, it is very unfortunate that until now giant agricultural industries are not yet as they should be in Egbe. It is only very recently that some plant industries (sawmills) are being established there, whereas substantial timber forests are found in Egbe. It is also sad to note that Egbe farmers lose a lot of their products due to lack of either small scale processing industries or conglomerate farm processing and preservation ventures. If these factories are not established plenty of food items will continue to rot away during the harvest seasons.

According to the Authors, the yearning of Egbe people is to appeal to both Federal and State Governments to come to her assistance through establishing agricultural industries in Egbe. In order to enhance this effectively, all season motor-able roads are required to link the various farms so that produce can be adequately transported to the processing points and consumers in other cities where the demand for these products are high. Egbe people therefore appeal to government agencies such as the Nigerian Agricultural Co-operative Banks (NACB), the National Agricultural Land Development Authority (NALDA), the Directorate of Food Roads and Rural Infrastructures and other parastatals to come to their aid. One of the net and positive results of government involvements in Egbeland would be to contribute significantly to rapid national development and food sufficiency. The challenge is great and it calls for prompt attention by both the government and the industrialists who can make fortunes through corporate agricultural ventures. The 'greenland farms' started some years back but many more investors are always invited to come and explore and take advantage of the latent agricultural potentials in Egbe.

Photograph 3 shows Egbe General Post Office while Photograph 4 depicts the Television Post which is located off Egbe-Kabba road. Photograph 5 depicts the old Egbe Town Hall located close to one of the many surrounding hills in the town. A map of Egbe and locations is provided in Exhibit 1 with the associated Key next to it. This contains the names of the various places identified. Unfortunately the map was not drawn to any precise scale but it will serve to assist those people who are unfamiliar with the town. A similar map was drawn by Olumotanmi (no date) when writing on the legacy of Titcombe College but the inscriptions on his map was too tiny to be legible.

Exhibit 2 presents a map of West Yagba local government area of Kogi State and it comprises several towns and villages notably: Egbe, Odo-Ere, Okere, Okunran, Ogbe, Ogga, Omi, Odo-Eri, Okoto, Iyamerin, Igbaruku, Odo-Ara, Ejiba and Isanlu-Esa. Again, the map was not drawn to scale but it will serve to assist those people who are unfamiliar with the local government area. From the exhibit, we can see, among other things that West Yagba local government area has several rivers and streams notably Oyi, Ofili, Otun, Ofe, Owuru and Lawiri. The map demarcates the state and local government boundaries as well as the major roads in the area.

Photograph 3: Egbe General Post Office

Chapter 1: Introduction

Photograph 4: Television Post (off Egbe-Kabba Road)

Photograph 5: Egbe Town Hall

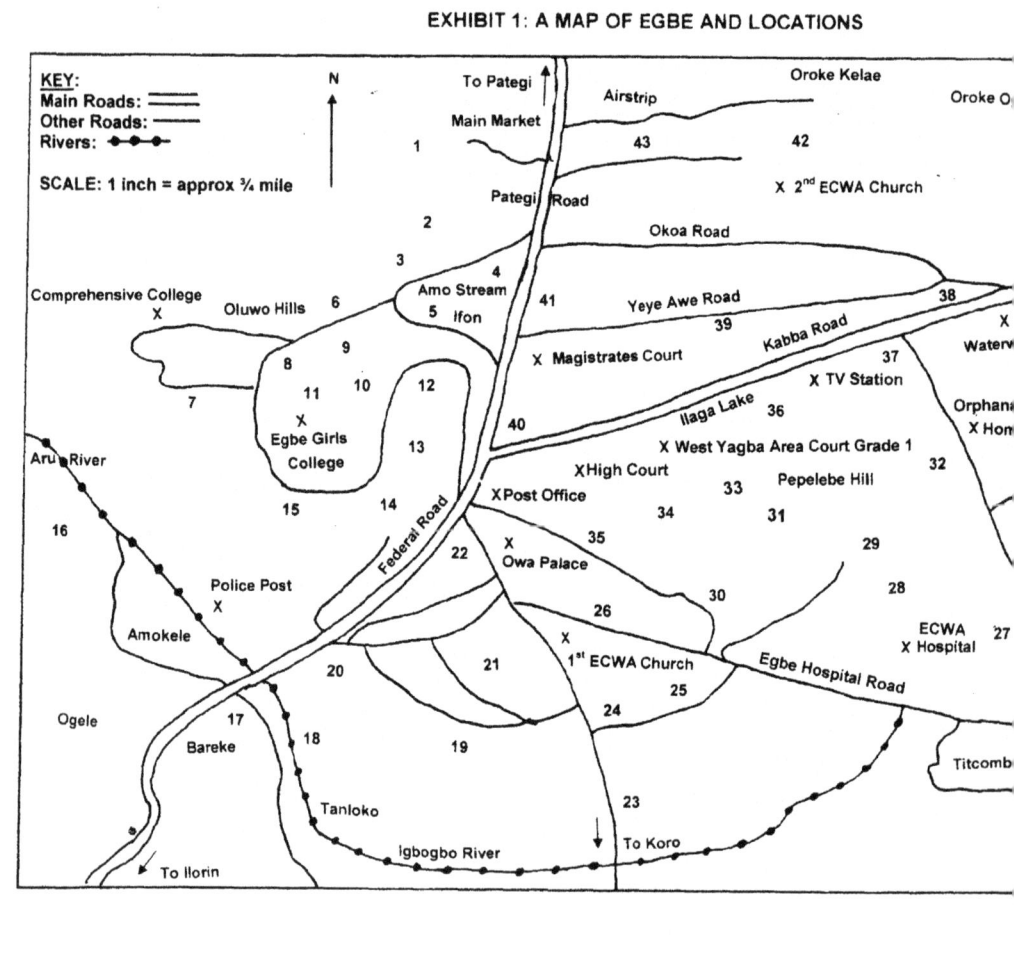

EXHIBIT 1: A MAP OF EGBE AND LOCATIONS

Key to Exhibit 1: A Map of Egbe and Locations
1. Kwara Radio
2. Saw Mill
3. Owojaiye Street
4. Government Hospital and Government Hospital Road
5. Ifon Road
6. Access Road
7. College Access Road
8. Ijalu Mountain
9. Church of God in Christ
10. Oluwo Mountain
11. Catholic Church
12. St Johns Primary School
13. Local Government Primary School
14. Salvation Artny Church
15. Salvation Army Primary School
16. Low Cost Federal government Housing
17. Federal Ministry of Works
18. Skyway Hotel
19. Fifth ECWA Church
20. Jehovah Witness Hall
21. Christ Apostolic Church
22. First Century Church
23. Koro Road
24. Maraba Road
25. Third ECWA Church
26. Ogba Onimosi Road
27. Egbe School of Nursing
28. Old Mission House
29. ECWA Central School
30. Mercy Clinic
31. First ECWA Church Cathedral
32. Ayin Oro Road
33. Rest House Clinic
34. First Bank
35. Church/Mission Road
36. Baptist Church
37. Fourth ECWA Church
38. Fetty Hotel

39. Mosque
40. Ajaforunti Triangle
41. Ajewo Palace
42. Egbe Government College
43. ECWA Schools

Chapter 1: Introduction

EXHIBIT 2: A MAP OF WEST YAGBA LOCAL GOVERNMENT AREA

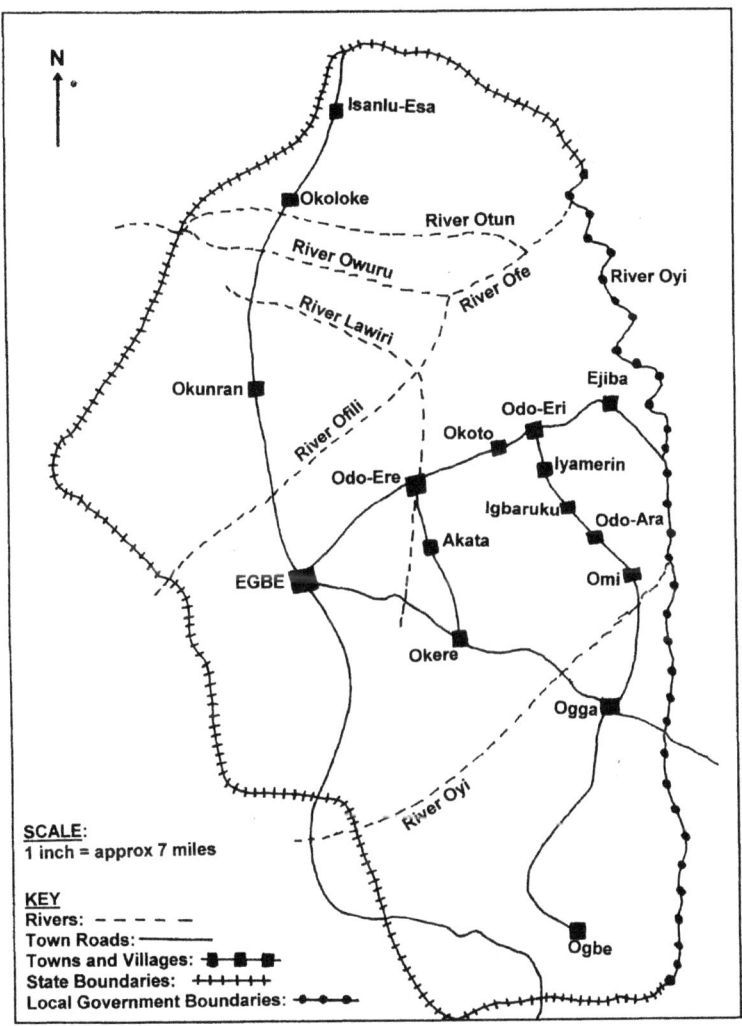

Chapter 2: Relationships with the Environs

Chapter Two discusses the origin and demarcation of Yagbaland, its relationship with the Nupes, the protest styled 'Mokobon Movement', Yagba Council and rivalry among Yagba towns and villages.

Bulifant (1950, p.26) described the Yagba people thus: 'The Yagbas are the most north easterly tribe living in Yorubaland. They are really part of the great Yoruba nation. Although they number only about seventy-five thousand, they have a dialect of their own'. Bulifant suggested that the early missionaries recognised the potential of Egbe in terms of population, strategic location, trade and commerce. She went on to suggest that Egbe was often referred to as the 'Lagos' of Yagba and explained that this was because of its proximity to western civilisation serving all Yagba, Igbomina and Ekiti districts of Kogi, Kwara and Ondo states (Bulifant, op. cit.).

Further explaining the demarcation of Yagbaland, oral historians said that the British colonial arrangement placed a section of the people i.e. the people of Egbe, Ejiba, Eri, Ogga and Okoloke areas, later known as West Yagba, in the Nupe-dominated Lafiagi-Pategi division of Ilorin province with its headquarters at Lafiagi. Ijagbemi explained that their counterparts in the Isanlu, Mopa, Orokere, Amuo, Ilae, Okeagi, Ejuku, Takete, Ife, Ponyan, Jege and Ogbom areas, later known collectively as East Yagba, were included as a district of Kabba division in a newly created Kabba province with its headquarters in Kabba town. Thus, according to Ijagbemi, the Yagba of Irele, Oke-Ako, Ipao, Itapaji, and Iye who were found in the South-West portion of Yagba land ended up in Aiyede district of Ondo province.

The Origin of Yagba
The origin of Yagba is legendary. The word is a contraction of two words Iya-Agba shortened to Yagba. An old woman reportedly migrated from old Oyo and her children, who were both hunters and farmers, formed settlements at different locations in Yagbaland. The early places of settlements include

Egbe, Eri, Ere, Ilae and later, Ife-Olukotun. There is an interesting legend explaining some of these early settlements. It was reported, for example, that on one occasion the three brothers of Iya-Agba were hunting together. One of them found an object in the trees in a location by which 'Eri' was derived. One of the other duo took the object and examined it at 'Ere' while the third brother decided to plant it at 'Egbe'. Yoruba readers will appreciate the literal interpretations of these words! While the credibility of the legend may be suspect, its significance is the fact that these towns were found by the three brothers of the same family of Iya-Agba. Thus the towns historically have a common ancestry.

In 1886, Yagba was a member of the Ekiti confederation. Later, Yagba opted out of the confederation and became independent. Before this development the confederation fought and Egbe participated for seventeen years in the notorious Okemesi wars where Egbe infantry was distinguished for its use of poisonous arrows. These arrows were reportedly deposited in a war house at Egbe in a place called Abidosi. At this time the Elere of Ere, Oba Iyewarun was the head of Yagba district. He was appointed in 1930 and had maintained an attitude of insolence and disloyalty to Etsu of Pategi for which he had been warned against on several occasions. While Oba Iyewarun was originally the popular choice he soon lost the support of his people through accusations of general incompetence and embezzlement of taxes. Consequently he was deposed in 1932.

Egbe is the largest community in Yagbaland and the capital of Yagba. While slave raiding occurred on its borders there was not a single occasion when Yagba was subjugated by invaders. Egbe itself was surrounded by thick and high walls and this made it impossible for invading armies to enter the fortified town. Writing about its role as a place of refuge, Kayode (2003) suggested that the hills and walls surrounding the town provided a safe shelter. According to him, 'the wall was as high as 12 to 20 feet above the outside level of the ground surrounded by a mote that was about 7 feet deep'. Thus Egbe had multiple earthen walls with deep ditches and high strong gates to protect her citizens. Security was therefore one attraction to Egbe as it became known as a town of refuge. Slaves who were able to free themselves from their captors or people running away from captivity in the first instance fled to Egbe and received protection. The political freedom gained by residents at Egbe also complemented their security from internecine wars as the town 'had no Ajele in it and was entirely subject to no power' (Simonyan, 1991, p.12).

Abraham Olokundun gave a list of several individuals from neighbouring towns and villages that were reported to have come to take refuge in Egbe during the wars. However the list is not published here in order to avoid controversy. It is believed that during slavery and intertribal wars Egbe saved many non indigenous sons and daughters from captivity within its strong walls. Actually the past role of Egbe infantry can be compared, in some respects, with the present role of Egbe Hospital in saving many lives.

Relationship with the Nupes
The relationship of the Yagba people with the Nupes was that of trade and commerce and it was a cordial and independent mutual business transaction. The relationship was strengthened by a devout Moslem traveler and scholar, Ida Chaba in 1830. He first went to Isanlu but returned to Egbe where he spent many years at Isaba which is often called a safe haven for refugees and the oppressed. Isaba was founded by a family of Okoa called Ile Elejo. The family broke up in a dispute to found Isaba. Ida Chaba stayed near a lake called Ilaga. The lake has provided water supply for the populace but due to lack of proper care the lake became infested with guinea worms and has been closed to the public for sometime. However the spring is still preserved as a shrine to the goddess of fertility.

Another contact with Egbe by a Nupe man was that of Masaba who lived in Egbe between 1843 and 1850. He was the ruler of Lade in Nupeland. He fled his homeland having been defeated in a battle at a place south of the River Niger by Etsu Umaru and Etsu Maza who were commanders in the Bornu army. Masaba lived in Egbe for many years but was called back to Nupeland by his subjects (Niven, 1957). Masaba was escorted back from Isaba compound in Egbe by a unit of Egbe infantry, armed with bows and poisonous arrows. With the assistance of the Egbe soldiers Masaba defeated his rival Etsu Umaru and his followers and regained his kingdom. Since that time onward there has been an exchange of annual gifts between the rulers of Egbe and Bida. According to oral historians the good relationship between Egbe and the Nupe people acted as a catalyst for contact with the rest of Yagba and other towns and villages in the Bunnu and Ijunmu areas.

During the slave trade era, there were attacks by the Nupe soldiers against less powerful towns and villages than Egbe but the Nupes found Egbe soldiers formidable. Several attempts were made by the Nupes to subjugate Egbe people but these attempts were rebuffed by the Egbe infantry. There was a story that the Nupes wanted to launch a surprise attack on Egbe town but the plan was detected and foiled as the Nupe army camped at Haragba only three miles away from the centre of the town. Oral history suggest that in the night Egbe spies entered the Nupe's military camp and dislodged the commander's bed and that of his spouse through magico-spiritual powers without waking them up! The next morning as the soldiers absconded they were frightened crying 'sogoyo', a Nupe expression of trepidation. The relationship between the two groups became sour when the colonial demarcation orders placed Yagba under Nupe's area of jurisdiction. That situation was regarded as unacceptable by the Egbe people so they fought and later on successfully had these orders reversed.

Protests and Mokobon Movement
The Mokobon Movement was organised as a rejection of the Nupe's rule by Egbe people. Mark Dada, the late Olu of Okeri and the district head of West Yagba in 1978 blamed the Yagba people for their care-free attitude that led to the imposition of the Nupe's rule upon them. Despite protests by the Yagba people the superior military might of the colonial authority suppressed the protests. The British, who were in full control of the situation, forced upon the Yagba people a highly detested Nupe sub-imperialism which was accompanied by a high degree of brutalisation. It was believed that the Yagba people, at least in the short run, had no choice but to resign themselves to their fate.

However the Mokobon Movement continued to be active with meetings and protest marches which the Chiefs and community leaders organised both privately and publicly. Protests erupted from these series of activities instigated by the Egbe people. It was reported also that the Yagbas, inspired by the Christian message of all human equality before God, came to loggerheads with the Nupe administration on the supposed superiority of the Nupes over them.

The Yagbas, represented by West Yagba Chiefs constituted a delegation led by the Asalu of Egbe in protest against the inclusion of the area under the Nupes. The people could not accept payment of taxes to the Nupes because of their independence prior to the colonial era. A series of meetings were held and protest marches were organised even to the seat of the administration in Pategi. The protest against Nupe rule was supported by the early missionaries who saw the injustices and the brutalities of the Nupe rule as abhorrent. Tommy Titcombe was personally involved with the uprising of the Yagbas against the oppressive rule of the Nupes. David Adeniyi together with Tommy Titcombe as well as other Yagba leaders met many times at Okutadudu in Odo-Ere and in Egbe. They also met in Lagos, Ibadan and other Yoruba towns to discuss the rejection of Nupe Rule. Encouragement was given by the late Herbert McCaulay and J K Randle. The political activities of the SIM, led by Tommy Titcombe in opposition to the repressive and brutal rule of the Nupes and the British displeased the British Colonial Administration, notably Lord Lugard.

In June 1930 the Resident of Ilorin accompanied by the District Officer and the Etsu of Pategi came to Egbe to announce an immediate creation of a United Yagba Council with a Yagba District Head as directed by the Colonial Administration from Lagos. From 1930 to 1934 the administrative structure for the district was re-organised and set up. Egbe became the headquarters for West Yagba after separation from Pategi Division. The village head of Ere, the Elere of Ere, Oba Iyewarun, became the first district head of West Yagba. His headquarters were installed at Egbe where he lived until his deposition in March 1932.

Yagba Council

Oba Iyewarun was called Oba Yagba and he lived at Oke Agada, a location near the first ECWA Church at Egbe. The Oba did not receive the necessary encouragement and support from both the Egbe people and from the Etsu of Pategi. It is suggested that had the Elere of Ere been accepted by the Egbe people, Egbe could have remained the headquarters for West Yagba. However, given the scramble for development opportunities the struggle inherent in the siting of West Yagba headquarters anywhere would have been acrimonious as each town or village would like its own chief, bank, hospital, college, etc. After the deposition of Oba Iyewarun Chief Eleworamo Fayomi Agbana became the ruler of Egbe and he was appointed as the district head of West Yagba.

On April 1, 1934 West Yagba was joined with East Yagba in a ceremony at Kabba. This marked the final collapse of the administrative relationship between the Yagba and Pategi colonial administration. Under the new arrangement there were village councils and two sub-district councils on the Yagba Council. The Aloko of Mopa and the Agbana of Egbe were the joint presidents of the council. The sub-district councils met once a month to coincide with a court sitting at Mopa or Egbe while the central council met once a quarter usually at Isanlu but occasionally at Egbe. Eleven members were appointed for each of the sub-district councils.

Clerks were appointed to each meeting. The first to be appointed was Abraham Olokundu, born in Opada compound, Egbe. He was one of the early converts to Christianity by Tommy Titcombe. Relieved of his post when on a tax assessment tour, without any charges, Oshagbemi, the father of David Oshagbemi, popularly known as Karaole, was appointed in his place. Just as his predecessor he was also on an assessment tour when he was relieved of his post and replaced by Samuel Olayemi (the father of Oladele Olayemi, current owner of a psychiatric hospital, at Ilorin, Kwara State). The police carried out the orders of employment and dismissal at the pleasure of the district head. The clerks had no formal training and were simply the products of Sunday school classes organised by Reverend Titcombe.

Rivalry among Yagba Towns and Villages

Hermon Hodge (1934, p.923) wrote about the administrative affairs of the natives of Yagbaland. He said that whenever he visited Yagba district he was usually met by a small deputation from one village or another, which claimed to speak for the people of Yagba. Such a deputation would normally request that their chief be made the district head. The reason for such a request was to demand a higher salary by the chief which would tend to refer to a higher status. Alternatively they may have requested an upgrading of their chief to a higher status that would automatically attract a higher salary and fringe benefits. Hodge also suggested that the truth is that there was not and never had been cooperation among members of the district for the common good. Each village would have liked to be completely independent from every other village and to have its own treasury, court, prison and so on. Even today this attitude remains a challenge to politicians from the area.

Hodge also suggested that the Yagba people indulged in political dreams and few council meetings passed without a request for a single chief of Yagbaland, although the people have admitted that they would be unable to agree on any one man. Contrary to the Yagba district meetings, the quarterly council meetings were always well attended and less ambitious schemes were discussed intelligently at those meetings.

Chapter 3: Common Beliefs and Practices

Chapter Three critically assesses the culture or the common beliefs and practices of Egbe people. We know that culture describes the values, traditions, norms, customs, arts, history, folklore, and institutions that a group of people, who are unified by race, ethnicity, language, nationality, or religion, share. It explains the accumulated habits, attitudes, and beliefs of a group of people that define for them their general behaviour and the total set of learned activities that they share. Egbe culture embraces indigenous traditions, moral education and artistic values and it permeates through generations and changes from time to time.

In this book we simply regard culture as a description of a people's way of life. The culture of Egbe people finds expression in various arrangements and practices of the people amongst which are for example their beliefs and rituals, initiation into womanhood, age grouping system ('Are'), traditional African religion and other beliefs and ways of life. These issues will be presented and discussed in this chapter.

Beliefs and Rituals

The people of Egbe believe in a supreme being called God, Oba Orun or Olorun. They are monotheists but they also believe in the existence of the lesser gods and deities who are thought to be intermediaries between God and man. These beliefs emanate from the community's perception of the world around them, the need for survival, security and the general welfare of the community. There are also beliefs in the cults of ancestors, divinities, herbalists, occult practices, priests, witches, secret societies, rainmakers and moon cults. Today, Egbe is a multicultural society with a variety of different religions. They believe in the existence of taboos, the violation of which could bring disaster to the community. Examples of such beliefs include not stretching one's hands out in the rain so as not to attract lightning and thunder and not talking at midnight to avoid inviting demons and ghosts! These beliefs are taught to the children in order to regulate their social behaviour in the community. The fear of what might happen tend to dissuade members from violating the taboos, beliefs and the superstitions no matter how stupendous some of them might appear!

When an individual dies, there is wailing by the members of the immediate and extended family system. In addition when the news breaks, there is normally feasting and singing to commemorate the passing away of the aged person to the life beyond, believed to be another and a better world. The latter activities take place a few days after the burial of the corpse. In short there is a belief of life after death. It is suggested that dead people can see and sometimes guide the living but that the living cannot see the dead. Implicitly therefore it is believed that the dead exist within communities of the living. Such a belief, while unchristian, is comparable with the Greek mythology of life after death, reflected in some Oriental beliefs. It is thought that those people who have died observe the living as they struggle through life often warning them to be cautious. The Egbe masquerade is the worship of ancestral spirits. The dead are believed to be capable of coming back to the world to assist the individual and the community as well as to punish the evil doer. There are sometimes stories of encounters with a dead person on her/his journeys in towns outside Egbe, far away in some ancient Yoruba towns or in some other parts of the country. In Ile-Ife there are places where Egbe indigenes do not go because of the fear of meeting dead relatives there. There is also a belief in the rebirth of the dead. Such a belief gives meaning or expression to names such as Oyejide, Yetunji, Biobaku, Babajide, Dehinde, etc.

In rituals concerning death, funeral rites are not performed for strangers, thieves, murderers, witches, troublemakers and those whose deaths are considered to be abnormal. The body of a dead person is washed with water or traditional medicine, rubbed with oil and cotton is placed in the nostrils, ears and other openings to prevent blood from oozing out from the body. White cloth and cotton are then used to wrap up the corpse while the body is anointed with perfume. Children, pregnant women or suspected witches are not allowed to be near a corpse. Burial is usually done on the same day although it tends to take longer these days with the provision of embalmment facilities at the Egbe hospital. When there is a written or oral will made before death, such wishes are always respected. For example one of the authors' mothers requested to be buried within three to seven days of death and her wish was carried out to the letter.

Traditionally, in the early 20th Century, the body of the dead person was buried with some of his/ her belongings. The belief was that the person would still avail herself or himself of those properties in the new world! Personal belongings buried with the dead person in the past may include such items as spears, stools, bows and arrows, ornaments, money, tools and domestic utensils. As indicated earlier, the belief is that the deceased persons may need the tools on their journeys into the world beyond. Funeral rites depend on the age, status and religious/professional associations of the deceased. Basically, a child's burial is simple and confined to relatives. The elderly people's funeral attracts friends and the extended family but for a Chief or a King it is the entire community that buries them. Wailings and lamentations are commonplace with the living listing and discussing the good things the deceased had done while on earth and how the war of survival would be difficult without the departed.

It is believed that manifestations of life after death appear in dreams or visions. The majority of dead people at Egbe are buried in the family burial ground specially built for the purpose. These are often not far away from the family living quarters. It is not unusual for some payments to be demanded by the birth family of a deceased married woman, to be made to the family into which she has been married before approval is given for them to bury the dead person in her place of choice. Any unilateral burial without prior clearance from the birth or natal family may precipitate the need to exhume the corpse in order to enforce the tradition. Normally, families have shrines where they expect each and all of their children to be buried. Once approval is obtained to bury a person outside her birth family home, however, both families take active parts in the burial rites and in the ceremonies.

There are beliefs in the existence of ghosts which are often said to appear in houses, on roads and in many other places.

They are said to be capable of moving very fast! The dead people are officially remembered in ceremonies or festivals which are full of dancing and feasting. Families honour this process, as indicated above, by naming new babies after them. A typical high profile burial ceremony would be accompanied with lavish expenses including the slaughtering of cows, the provision of plenty of food, specially made clothes, drinks and invitations to guests. It is said that the emphasis and huge expenses often spent on a burial ceremony are sometimes inversely related to the respect and care accorded the victim when alive. There were rituals in the olden days which were ceremonial in situations such as birth, war, raids, locust invasion or in the case of a natural calamity like devastating storm. The 'Akefun' in Egbe is performed to expel evils that may threaten the community. Women dress up as if they are men going to war. The nature of the sacrifice to be performed would normally have been foretold by a diviner. It is believed that the practice of these rituals is advantageous to the unity of the community.

There are several personal rituals performed during the life of a person and these include, naming ceremony, puberty, circumcision, initiation, engagement, marriage, pregnancy, childbearing, old age, death, etc. Other non personal rituals include agricultural and hunting rites which are performed for better farm yields and success at hunting and fishing for a family. Rituals are performed on new farm lands to drive away evil spirits and to make them very productive! The community often invites rain makers to facilitate rainfall during a dry year and large sums of money may also be paid to diviners for sacrifices of dogs, pigs and cattle by the whole community for similar objectives. The materials for rituals include domestic crops, roots and leaves while flowers are used for purification and the prevention of harm to individuals and to promote blessings.

As the life of an adult usually involves engagement at some point, rituals are performed to smoothen this. In the traditional society the Ifa Oracle is consulted to give prediction for the future of an intending couple. The couple is investigated to find out whether there are maladies which are hereditary in either families such as epilepsy, mental illness or any irresponsible antisocial behaviour like bankruptcy or theft. Certain rites and sacrifices that are dictated by the diviner are complied with so as to avert any future potential problems. It is during the engagement that the families of the girl ask the families of the boy to pay certain items such as kola nuts, a pig, a brown she goat, kegs of palm wine or a carton of beer, etc. A mini family party is held after which the boy and girl are pronounced married. After a traditional engagement a couple may go ahead and have children even if they are not married (in the western sense). The marriage ceremony itself can take place at any time even after the couple may have had a number of children. Engagement appears to be what is required in the traditional society. With relative affluence these days, however, most couples perform both ceremonies.

In the past there used to be what is popularly known today as 'an arranged marriage'. Steps were taken by a man's parents to consult the parents of a girl and ask for her hand in marriage on behalf of a son who may be away in Lagos or in the northern part of the country. If asked, the father may pay the dowries for a wife on behalf of his son or more likely ask the son to come home and pay this himself. Gifts are exchanged during wedding ceremonies but the traditional demands of the family of the lady would include yams, palm oil, dried fish, salt, pepper, kola-nuts and honey. When the dowry is paid this is shared among the family members, including the parents, sisters and brothers of the bride. It is necessary to state here that a wife is not considered married solely to her husband as practised in the western world but a wife is regarded as married to the family of the partner. The wife respects or is expected to respect each member of the husband's extended family who she will not call by their names but address them as 'mother', 'father', 'brother', 'sister', 'husband', 'wife' and so on.

Initiation Into Womanhood
'Ifon' is the tradition of initiating maidens into womanhood. This is done by the bathing of maidens at Ilaga shrine, a lake in Isaba. Maidens bathe only once before they go to Amo where they perform some traditional ceremonies. Ilaga and Amo are springs that are also regarded as shrines. It was believed that at

Amo you have the abode of the goddess of fertility called 'Yeye Lamo'. At 'Ifon' forest the hair of the maidens were shaved and their entire bodies rubbed with specially prepared brown ointment called 'Osun'. All these symbolise doing away with the old ways of life and entering into a new life of fertility. The maidens then return to their respective homes in white clothes and are forbidden from talking to anybody on the way. The would-be wives then go for three months (called moons) in the fattening homes only to be visited by their husbands and the experienced mothers who teach the maidens how to be good wives. After three months the would-be wives go with their maids to shop in the main market. This symbolises attainment of maturity.

There are three shrines the would-be wives must enter to receive the blessings of the goddess of fertility. They are the Illaga lake, Ifon bush and Amo spring. The 'Ifon' is comparable with the 'fattening system' in Calabar, where young girls are kept in fattening rooms and trained by experienced mothers on how to be good housewives. Those who go through the 'fattening system' are said to be indigenes of Egbe of the old order. They are called 'Omo Owu'. The Omo Owus migrated from Egbe to other places in Yagba and Ekiti lands and even beyond. The places where the Omo Owus migrated to include, but are not limited to, the following: Isanlu, Mopa, Ponyan, Ejuku, Jege, Ife-Yagba, Ejiba, Ere, Ogbe, Obbo-Aiyegunle, Ilesha, Abeokuta, Ijebu, etc.

Indigenous elders often demonstrate nostalgia for their homeland in statements such as: 'Woriwo gho omo Owu tu wo oja Egbe yeni gbon aso re'. The meaning of the statement is that the nudity with which Owu's children enter the Egbe market is more befitting than clothes. The practice encourages and applauds sexual morality before marriage. While nudity is, of course, obsolete in the current cultural practices, descendants still have its reminiscence especially in the context of the morality or the lack of it in modern days. The last day of the ritual is usually a visit to the Egbe Main Market. The bride's maid would carry the bag and other products purchased from the market for the new bride who has a special outfit to distinguish her as the bride. This ceremony is usually performed close to but before her actual wedding.

Age Grouping System ('Are')

The age-grouping system is a specific example of indigenous education. The system is prominent in Yagbaland but variants of this practice exist in other West African countries. Age-groupings are initiation rites sometimes of a highly formalised and institutionalised nature. The authors say that 'Are' incorporated apprenticeship schemes and that it assimilated to itself a certain measure of adult education in the pursuit of community development and leisure interests. It is important to realise that each system had specific forms of preparing individuals for their roles in society.

Fafunwa's (1980) description suggests that age grouping takes place every two years but at some places in Yagbaland the system could last three or more years in duration. In Egbe, for example, it takes place every nine years. This is the duration by which a group is promoted to a higher rank. The Egbe system comprises a range of activities that 'Are' people perform, including defense and internal administration of the town. Sometimes, at Egbe, the interval of nine years may be altered due to unexpected circumstances like, war, political or social problems. The present threat to the continuation of the age grouping system is the rise of a clique of elites who have had little or no cultural links to Egbe and who would like the culture to be obliterated under the guise of modernisation. Even without the expressed abandonment of the system, the realities of modern day life make the wholesome practice of the institution very unlikely in the future. Indeed many of these practices already appear to be crumbling down.

Today, the age grouping system still persists although in a modified and shortened form. In the past a period of three months was spent in the bush (school) for training and communal duties. Rituals and initiation rites were performed to ensure each pupil attained maturity with specific roles to be performed for the community. See Table 2. The town's philosophers, teachers and priests along with the council of elders participate in the ceremony. The chief priest called

'Aworo' is the only one who advances to take the shrine. Oral traditions suggest that, on each occasion, the chief priest would let lose a cow and then turn his back on the shrine. The adherents believed that a mysterious god would have slaughtered and cooked the whole cow within a few minutes! All the meat is consumed within the vicinity and it is a taboo to take any part of the meat into the town. Normally these activities are male dominated and the women are not allowed to feature in the ceremonies.

The chief priest was reported always to receive the prophecy for the next nine years after the offering of the cow. The anxious crowds gathered in compounds, open places and the market square to listen. The booming of the guns from the hills heralded the receipt of the prophecy by the chief priest and this is always in poetic forms. All the graduates in a particular year formed a single line, each holding a white cow's tail and a long stick on the right hand with a dried fish with charms and a parrot's feather attached to the long stick. Each participant wore a white loincloth. The parade was conducted into the main market of the town in a single file in a dance of trot and jump rhythmic steps to match the beating of metal bells. The ceremony lasted for a total of three months, i.e. three moons after which feasting took place in each graduate's house in turns. It should be understood that in Egbe the 'Are' ceremony took place only once every nine years.

Table 2 summarises 'Are' – the age-group system practices where an eight year interval is used from one 'Are' to the other.

Chapter 3: Common Beliefs and Practices

Table 2: Egbe Age Group System ('Are')

Group description	Age in years	Functions/ Vocations
Youngsters	05-13	Town cleaning and moral training
Middle-Age group	14-22	Physical training, gymnastics, wrestling, military training
Third group	23-31	Soldiers
Fourth group	32-40	City defenders, rescue operations while soldiers retreat
Fifth group	41-49	Administrators, philosophers, senior citizens
Six group	50-58	Treasurers and Judges
Seventh group	59-67	Advisors and chiefs are selected from the seventh to the twelfth groups of fathers or elders. These groups tend to be collapsed into one in practice to give an impression of only seven groups overall.
Eighth group	68-76	
Ninth group	77-85	
Tenth group	86-94	
Eleventh group	95-103	
Twelfth group	104-112	
Sources: Awarun, (1975), Awe, (1958).		

Table 3 documents 'Are' practices and activities from 1830 to date stating the title of each project executed, the accompanying predictions or affirmations and the interpretations of the philosophies of the Egbe people during each period.

Table 3: 'Are' Practices and Activities, 1830-2005

Dates	Title project/ prediction	Interpretation of position
1830	Egbe ke lojo	Re-building of city walls despite heavy rainfall, necessitated by the menace of invading inter-tribal warriors.
1838	Egbe ke ji	Egbe was unshaken despite threats of invasion as a reprisal for hosting Masaba, a refugee from Bida.
1846	Egbe ke sojo	No fear of invasion.
1854	Egbe emi do	No discouragement, no fear of any attack.
1862	Egbe ke maru	No fear of invasion as Masaba was followed to Bida with Egbe infantry and was re-instated to his office.
1870	Egbe ke loran	Egbe city gates allowed refugees from other towns and villages from many parts of Yorubaland when the Nupe people attacked them.
1886	Egbe e lojo	Egbe was not afraid because of threats of tribal wars from the Nupe and Ekiti-Parapo when Egbe took a leading role.
1894	Egbe ke jido	A general period of inter-tribal wars – Egbe was prepared.

Year	Name	Description
1902	Egbe ke Iohun	Egbe would not be discouraged by the Okemesi wars where she and Yagba fought for nine years.
1910	Egbe ke wahin	Nupe's attack was repulsed, slaves were captured, slave raids were perpetrated by Egbe and there was a feeling of security and independence.
1918	Egbe ke mo	British rule in collaboration with Tommy Titcombe freed the slaves and imposed an alien rule taking the Egbe people unaware. It was a period of conscription into forced labour gangs for the construction of roads. It was an era of regret, as Egbe domain was divided and isolated.
1926	Egbe ke seyo	There was a revolt against the British colonial administration that put Egbe under Nupe rule.
1942	Egbe e ti ko	Egbe had not been united causing problems of unity such as the deposition of Owa, the Agbana.
1950	Egbe e seji	This was an era of campaign for unity as more schools were built and roads rehabilitated. The Northern Nigeria Government approved 'Ajewo' palace for the whole of West Yagba – work started in 1953. The local education authority primary school was built in 1957. Titcombe College was built in 1951. Egbe Hospital, Nurses Training School, and the Post Office were built in 1953.
1958	Egbe ke ja	A period of cooperation; a postal agency built by communal labour was converted to an Education Office in 1959.
1966	Egbe ke sin	Egbe wanted political authority within the framework of the Federal Government. It was granted a town council status.
1974	Egbe ma dun	Facilities for the enjoyment of the community were multiplied at Egbe including expansion of the local market, construction of public water, rehabilitation of Egbe road, building of Egbe Girls College, building of the local dam and airfield and the supply of electricity.
1985	Egbe e sojo	Egbe was not afraid to fight the powers that stood against its faster development. There was a court action against the State Governor, Adamu Atta, on the siting of West Yagba Headquarters, and there were land disputes with neighbours. Egbe would not succumb to threats.
1994	Egbe gbisi	Egbe status is high.
2005	Egbe mayowa	Egbe has brought in joy.

Sources: Awarun, (1975), Awe, (1958).

Traditional African Religion

The indigenous religion in Egbe is a belief in mysticism such as the existence of ghosts, spiritual forces, witches, sorcerers, the gods and a supreme being God. The spiritual forces are appeased by supplications for support and to affect desired occurrences either currently or in the future. In every aspect of daily life the traditionalists consult the diviner for guidance. The spirits are invoked as a catalyst for the prepared medicines which are believed to be magical as they are effective and lead to healing. Recently some scholars have found it difficult to accept the validity of African indigenous religion. These religions were often very many and could include, for example, an earth cult, an ancestral cult, a divine cult, medicine cults, a witch cult, and several other cults. Each of these could be described as an institution since they consisted of a set of related beliefs, practices and attitudes which were administered by defined groups or sets of persons who may be said to embody the institution. The important question is about the usefulness of these cults and their medicines. Given the high mortality rates in Africa generally, not much could or can be said to support the potency of these 'miraculous' medicines.

While the essence of religion is the acknowledgement of the existence and worship of God, traditional African religion operates in a rather unique way in terms of its practice of libation and its respect for blood. There is the belief that the human soul originated directly from God and that blood is life. Therefore blood is revered because it is believed to be life itself. The shedding of blood unnecessarily, such as occurs during an abortion, is frowned upon in the traditional African society.

Deities or gods are identified with physical features such as hills and rivers. Hills are generally believed to contain wild animals and spirits known as 'iwin'. Hills also served as places of refuge during the intertribal wars. Rivers, especially larger ones, are regarded as important as they are believed to contain what is known as 'mammy water' and naiads. Some rivers such as Lawiri, Ilaga, Amo, Ofili and Apara are feared as people do get drowned in them. It is believed that this happens when the gods are angry. As usual, in order to appease the gods, sacrifices such as a chicken, a dog or any other animal requested by Ifa Oracle are offered. Spirits are believed to exist in large masses of water and these spirits are often worshipped as goddess of fertility.

This was true of Yeye Lamo, the mammy water in Amo Spring, where the water flow is perennial. It was believed that

Yeye Lamo had countless children and often gave to whosoever wanted. In consideration of this the stream is regarded as sacred. While would be wives who are virgins may go and bathe there before marriage there is a spot where no one is allowed to step on with their shoes. Olokun, the goddess of the seas, is believed to be extremely rich and the sacrifices that were offered to it ranged from white cloth to any bird or type of animal. A lady in need of a child would often make sacrifices to appease Olokun who was believed to have many children and would often give to those who ask her.

Other Beliefs and Practices

In this section we will discuss the following subtopics in sequence: the extended family system, traditional medicine, tribal marks, marriage, traditional dancing, sexual stratification, names, libation, praise chants and indigenous education. It is admitted, though, that there may be other issues or subtopics that may be of interest in the exploration of culture, beliefs and practices of the traditional Egbe people especially in contrast to the culture that they practise more often in today's world.

The extended family system is practised widely in Nigeria beyond Egbe or Yagbaland. It is a system that recognises human relationships beyond those in the typical nuclear family system – the mother, father, brothers and sisters – to include obligations to uncles, aunts, nieces, nephews, in-laws, cousins, etc. in the larger or extended family system. Close and distant relations are recognised for some assistance, if and when a need arises. In essence Yagbas are their brothers' keepers where extended family problems tend to be shared but so are family fortunes. Unfortunately there are problems with the practice of the extended family system as it sometimes results in fighting and recrimination amongst family members. This may not be unconnected with the fact that there tends to be more problems to share than fortunes.

Traditional medicine is normally prepared with certain ingredients like herbs, roots, sand, parts of animals and birds. All herbs have names by which they are identified by the herbalist. A typical African herbalist's medicine is packed in the animal's horn. To use it the spirits are invoked with some incantations.

Chapter 3: Common Beliefs and Practices

This can be used to conjure a curse or a blessing. In homeopathy an effigy may be prepared. This can be made of mud, wood or other materials. It is believed that whatever damage is done to the effigy prepared signals the harm that would be done to the enemy. It should be pointed out that the effigy would be infested with supernatural medicine and it is not just composed of ordinary wood or mud as it may appear. It was believed that similarly one's footprints could be harmed with devastating effect by an individual who steps on a wrong spot. Such a practice was used to harm or arrest thieves in the past. Certain herbs when incised into the feet were also believed to be capable of killing snakes when they are stepped upon. Needless to state, today, such beliefs are not popular.

Hunters were believed to use such medications a lot. Snakes are believed to be driven away with the smell of the herb placed on an individual with snake immunity. Various kinds of medicines used for protection against evil doers, wild animals, witches and sorcerers include amulets and charms. These are believed to perform magic when used as their functions are supposed to be mystical. Most medicines are effective when mixed with food and may be used to charm individuals and dogs such that for example captors may use it to dictate to the captives. It is claimed that lovers can be separated and rulers can be removed and dislodged by the use of these charms. Given the fact that some people have died, and still die, of poisonous snake bites in these regions, obviously the potency of some of the snakebite medicines used is suspect.

In the past the Yagba people were distinguished by three long tribal marks on each cheek far apart behind, but converging to a point at an angle near the mouth. The essence of the tribal mark was for identification purposes especially during the internecine wars and slavery. The practice of having tribal marks was very common in other parts of Nigeria such as Benin, Ogbomosho, Oshogbo, Ibadan, Igalaland, Nupeland and other parts of Nigeria and indeed, Africa in general. Today while the elderly people still carry the marks the practice has become obsolete with the modern Yagba people. Very few people still follow the tradition even in the remote places of Africa.

The traditional or customary marriage or marriage under native law at Egbe gives room for as many wives as the husband pleases and as many as he can afford. There are no legal restrictions against polygamy. Usually the circumstances, wants and means of a husband determine how many wives he has. In the past a strong man with a large farm may desire many children. While the girls would be available to harvest the crops the boys would till or dig the soil and perform other functions depending on their ages or physical strength. In inheritance a wife cannot inherit the property of her late husband as she can herself be inherited by a member of the extended family! The system, in its pure form, appears to leave a widow and her children to suffer but there are often interventions by some senior family members to minimise hardship as a result of her husband's death. Egbe practises the patrilineage family system which tends to favour the boys as they inherit their father's properties and extend their lineage through their own sons. The girls are married away into other families and they cannot, on their own, extend their father's lineage.

In the past traditional dancing was a communal act, anticipated, recognised and experienced by the audience and performers. It satisfied the functions of religious rituals, for example, in cases of the Sango of Ilemla or the Orisa of Ijagan. Apart from serving as a form of recreation dancing also serves as a social organisation designed to warn and expose wrong doers in the society. During the Igbemo dance, for example, some evil doers were publicly abused in songs around the town. Consequently dancing as a social organisation is used to safeguard the traditionally established social order and therefore the standards of expected behaviour and morality within the society are moderated by it.

Traditional dancing in Egbe has been an integral part of the society. Here the form and the motivation of the dance are familiar to all members of the society as it is part of their cultural heritage. There were indeed those members who could interpret the words and the messages of the talking drums! The traditional way of the movements and the standard associated with the dances can easily be assessed by the spectators who are familiar with the dances. Although there are innovations and modernisations in the instruments used there is the retention of customary performances which distinguish the traditional dance from the theatrical or modern day dances.

There is some sexual stratification at Egbe and in general, at most areas of Yagbaland. Girls are taught to be obedient to their husbands and taught the quality and value of chastity and morals. Sex before marriage was regarded as demeaning the good name of a responsible woman. Relations of a woman's husband are generally not called by their names; instead they are referred to as uncles and aunts by the woman. This is regarded as a form of respect. Strangely enough, to an outsider, even women of the husband's relations are referred to as 'husbands'. Where there is a polygamous home with children from other members of the family they must not be called by their names but are often referred to as uncle, aunt, husband, daddy or mother as may be deemed appropriate. A husband generally has the prerogative of being an overlord and almost incapable of wrong doing but he also has the responsibility of maintaining his household and providing for their needs through his hard work. Of course, in the present day Egbe society, the couple have equal rights in the home. It is important to observe that, while in yesteryears the girls used to stay at home and perform domestic activities, the boys would usually follow their fathers to the farm or to the bush to hunt for animals. The girls, on the other hand, tend to be more involved as traders with their mothers. In this modern day, however, things are different.

It is believed that every person has two names, the natural name and the given name. The natural name is believed to be brought from heaven and it explains the circumstances of a person's birth. Thus, twins, or those born after them, have natural names. Examples of some natural names for twins and those born in their nuclear families include Oke, Taiwo, Kehinde, Idowu, Taiye, Ige, Alaba and Aduke. As indicated earlier while natural names are understood to be given from heaven given names are chosen by the parents of a child and often, by the grandparents as well. However, given names or family names may also have some deeper meaning in terms of explaining the circumstances of the parents and what the birth of a child symbolises for them.

While the earth is believed to be subservient to the heavens the earth is worshipped because it yields fruits and crops for human sustenance. The suitable sacrifice here is libation whereby food and drinks are put on the ground supposedly to invoke the spirits. As most people depend on the crops from the soil, farmland is regarded as special. Problems such as pests, soil infertility and drought are confronted through worshipping the farmland. It is believed that yields are improved and famine is avoided through such worship. Harvest time is normally a time for celebration. For example, the new yam festival is celebrated annually in June and new yams are officially not eaten or taken to the market for sale until the festival is celebrated.

Oriki connotes praise chants and heroic actions intended to be emulated by posterity. Oriki helps to preserve records of the good past and spurs on listeners to greater achievements by their recitals. It is often recited on occasions such as marriage and chieftaincy ceremonies.

In Egbe the poetic citation of the general oriki i.e. the common praise chant, is 'Egbemekun Ojokedo'. This praise chant is a rallying symbolic force with motivating power to move people into action. 'Egbemekun' means the offspring of Tiger which instils bravery and fearlessness in the pursuit of societal good. It has been said that what 'harambe' means to the Kikuyus of Tanzania, 'Mekun' means to Egbe indigenes, Hiskett (1975). 'Ojo Kedo' says that those who fear in trepidation do not settle in Egbe.

For example, the chant associated with Pepelebe hill in Egbe reads thus:

Pepelebe were adiro,
Oroke o gbe ajogun a mo gbe orile,
Ijo ogun ba de, a dile. Oroke e dile, oniyan ri dile.

The chant means that Pepelebe is a relation to 'adiro'. When invaders start war, the oroke supports the invaders and not its citizens and hence it becomes 'flat' in order to assist the invaders. This signifies that it is people who become 'flat' by not supporting a cause and generally not physical structures during crises.

Chapter 3: Common Beliefs and Practices

It should be stated that many of the traditions explained appear to be of less importance today with multiculturalism and the influence of Christianity. Perhaps it should also be stated that Tommy Titcomb (yes, notice the spelling!) married Ethel Tucker on 15 November 1915 in Egbe. It was after the marriage that the letter 'e' was added to Titcomb**e**. The couple had three children. Clarence Herbert Titcombe was born on 15 December 1917 in Egbe. Edith Mary Titcombe and Emerson Peter Titcombe were twins born on 29 March 1919 in Hamilton Ontario, Canada. There were no known twins in the family before their arrival. They were born after much prayer because of the belief in Egbe at that time that twins had to be destroyed for fear that they possessed evil spirits. When the twins and their mother came back to Egbe the people saw that the twins and their mother were doing well, in good health and growing normally. This occasion made the Egbe people to change their prior belief that having twins was a curse!

Emerson became a medical doctor. His mind was geared towards being an academic medical practitioner. Clarence did not enjoy school much but he loved to draw and so he followed his passion for art and he was well known as a water-colour artist. Ethel, their mother, was a nurse. Diane Martin who lives in Vancouver, Canada is the grand daughter of Tommy Titcombe. The descendants of Tommy Titcombe still live in Canada.

Despite the introduction and growth of Western education in Egbe, indigenous education co-exists, to a large extent, and is reflected in the home, the community and the institutions. This is because indigenous education is fundamental and it is part of the lifestyle and practices of the people.

In the traditional society informal education starts early at infancy. This is when the young ones are made aware of such things as heat, filth, and sharp objects. The learning process involves listening, watching, imitating and repeating statements, songs or threats. Gradually the child advances into playing with other children in groups. When a child is about four years old he or she performs activities with his/her peer group and they are taught societal norms by the more elderly ones. At an early age the care of a child becomes a matter for the extended family system rather than that of the nuclear family alone as in the

Western culture. Any adult in the family may be involved in discouraging bad habits such as sucking one's fingers, greed and pilfering. At the same time the adults may organise some play groups telling the children stories with morals, sharing with them riddles, folklores, proverbs and taboos. These encourage informal learning to take place.

Respect for the elders is enforced by requiring the male children to prostate and the female children to kneel down when greeting chiefs, irrespective of their ages, or other people who maybe as old as their parents. Such norms are enforced from about the age of eight through to sixteen years. Threats, taboos and superstitions are attached to the anti-social behaviours. For example, it might be said that whoever disrespects an elder will die young! Similarly the social system operates through the encouragement of rewards just as it does with the threat of punishment. For example, well-behaved children may be blessed by elders just as poorly-behaved ones may be cursed by them.

From an early age children tend to be separated in their duties based on their gender. Girls fetch water with their mother, clean the rooms and the compound, prepare meals, wash dishes, gather firewood and buy things in the market and so on. The boys, on the other hand, go to the farms with their fathers, till the soil, reap the crops, kill bush animals and generally engage in the similar activities that their fathers do. Thus, the children learn from their parents the responsibilities of adulthood. In a family where there are no girls the boys perform all domestic duties although girls do not generally go with their fathers to the farms. One exception is when it is time to reap the crops. Girls do not till the soil as the boys do although in some other parts of Nigeria, girls may have a custom of tilling the soil.

Children and the young ones also go with their parents to attend various ceremonies and festivals and generally acquaint themselves not only with the economic but also the social and cultural norms of their locality. These activities may be regarded as informal education. For example, a youngster normally shares, food, fruits or meat amongst a group and allows the elders within that group to choose before the child does.

Some children are specifically selected by their parents to undertake certain jobs. A favourite child or a child who is being groomed for a leadership role within the society may be chosen to accompany especially, his father, to various appointments, meetings, ceremonies and festivals. This would give him the opportunity to become acquainted with the aphorisms of the aged and certain fixed events in the community calendar. A child who is knowledgeable about the traditions and practices of their people is a potential candidate for leadership positions within the community.

The apprenticeship system is one in which the child is socialised to a work role and the system is a viable economic aspect of indigenous education. The system helps to alleviate the problems of unemployment and it also assists individuals to fit into society as it is responsive to local needs. Some trades taught during the apprenticeship system include bakery, printing, photography, motor mechanics, electrical work, dry cleaning, carpentry and building.

While the employment of the apprentices in work not directly within the trade they want to learn may be seen by some people as exploitative, the apprentices themselves generally do not see things that way. This is because they not only eat in the house of their masters they also tend to broaden their learning in related activities. Hence they are happy to run errands and undertake petty trades for their masters. In some vocations identified with particular families concern is exercised by an ageing master to identify and groom a successor in good time before he or she retires.

Photograph 6 depicts Oluwo hill or Oroke Ijalu. It was taken from Ilorin/Kabba/Pategi junction close to the Ajaforunti sculpture. The same Oluwo, Oroke Ijalu, is taken from close proximity in Photograph 7.

Photograph 6: Oluwo, Oroke Ijalu taken from Ilorin/Kabba/Pategi junction

Photograph 7: Oluwo – Oroke Ijalu

Chapter 4: Chieftaincy Institutions

Chapter Four introduces the history of chieftaincy institutions in Egbe. It specifies the traditional ruling houses for Owa, the highest traditional title, in chronological order until the present time. It discusses the origin of Owa and itemises all the 'Akus' in the town indicating where Owa can be appointed. It also indicates, in a table format, the traditional titles at Egbe, their origins and functions. The decline in the current status of Owa is alluded to and this is explained, in part, as a result of the inevitable modernisation in today's world.

A brief account of the role of Tommie Titcombe in Egbe politics is given and this is followed by a description of Egbe chiefs from 1914 until the present time. The names of the four most recent chiefs in chronological order of the time they came to power are: Oba Aina Owojaiye, Oba Joseph Babalola Denki, Oba James Oluremilekun Adegboyega Olokundu and Oba Stanley Kayode Owa. The institution and the role of honorary chiefs are also briefly looked at.

History

Owa was the highest chieftaincy title in Egbe and it is still the highest title there today among the traditional chiefs. Owa originated from Okoa and was confined to Okoa for 35 consecutive occasions. It moved to Ijagan only during the 36th installation when a woman was enthroned. Since then, the title has rotated amongst Okedisin, Isaba and Okoa clans respectively. To date, the name of the last Owa to rule is Marku Oni, an indigene from Ijagan. Since his death in 2005, a successor is yet to be appointed. The table below shows the ruling houses in Egbe, where the Owas came from and the number of installations to date.

Table 4: Owas and the Ruling Houses

Ruling Houses	Owas of Egbe
Okoa	35 cases
Ijagan	1st case
Okedisin	1 case
Isaba	1 case
Okoa	36th case
Ijagan	2nd case (died in 2005)

The history of Owa cannot be fully appreciated without due reference to Okoa, where it originated. 'Okoa' is a contracted word meaning 'Owa's Spear'. As the chiefs met frequently to discuss societal matters e.g. war and community development, Owa had the last say. As Owa strikes his spear into the ground, it signifies a final decision on issues especially those dealing with societal protection and wars.

Origin of Owa
Awe Kati narrated the history of Owa to one of the authors in 1958. The first Owa was Kelae, a prince from Old Oyo Empire, who lost the claim to the stool of Alafin to his younger step brother (refer to Chapter 1 where this point was made). In order to avert physical conflict he decided to leave Oyo for a new settlement. From the narrated history, Owa of Ilesha was his uncle and he vainly persuaded Kelae to return to his domain. Owa of Ilesha and Kelae then made a pact that they would not attack each other. Thereupon Kelae was given a crown, an insignia of office locally called 'adirifun'. Unfortunately, the crown was said to have been stolen by the woman who became Owa and this insignia was buried with her in Ijagan. Consequently, subsequent Owas have to go to Ijagan to swear an oath of allegiance to the Office.

There was a different story explaining why there was a change of dynasty from Okoa to Ijagan. The alternative story suggests that the reigning Owa had three sons and a daughter. It was a customary practice that the reigning Owa gave the insignia of office to his favourite son. But on this particular occasion, the female child was reportedly very close to the ailing

Owa while the Owa's three male children did not care for him. Therefore, the Owa gave the insignia of office to the daughter before he died. The three male children then ganged up to prevent her installation but they failed. There was turmoil and disturbances that attracted the attention of the community. At the settlement, community members vowed never again to allow Okoa alone to have Owa's title as its prerogative. It was at that point in chieftaincy history that efforts culminated in the demand for participation in what was the exclusive prerogative of the Okoa clan. It would be observed from Table 4 that unlike in the first 35 cases, other rulers came from the different areas of Egbe.

Owa was the highest and Alaofin (Alafin) was the oldest chieftaincy title in the town. Alafin was confined to Oke Aofin of Okoa, Ogbaroko, Odorom, Aofin and Odoogba. Kelae gave this title to his younger brother who was in charge of all Egbeland. Owa ruled with the advice of a council of chiefs. The chiefs had control on certain matters in their areas of jurisdiction depending on the rank of a particular chief in the hierarchy (Olaniyan, 1982). All that Kelae did was to have a similar system in Egbe reminiscent of old Oyo and Ile-Ife. The Ekitis and the Igbominas of Kwara State are said to have similar chieftaincy titles.

There are some positions with senior and junior incumbents. This is exemplified with Olu where we have Olu Kekere, junior chief, and Olu Agba, senior chief. The same situation also applies to Olore Agba and Olore Kekere.

Obayemi (1986) explained the nature of the titles of village heads, 'Oba' or king and that village heads are rulers or owners of a particular settlement. Whilst in Yorubaland the terminology for chieftaincy is 'Olu', in Egbe, 'Olu' would normally be applied to the ward head and was never meant to be a head chief or the Oba of Egbe. As indicated earlier Owa is the title for the highest traditional chief in Egbe. It should be noted that Egbe was liberal in the award of chieftaincy titles and often had the title Ejio, to represent a chief for non-indigenes such as Mark Ejio of Okeleri who migrated from Okoloke.

Table 5: Chieftaincy Institution in Egbe

Name of 'Aku'	Entitlement to Owa of Egbe?	Entitlement to Oba of Egbe?	Entitlement to traditional chieftaincy title in Egbe?	Entitlement to Ikota (King Makers)?	Within old city wall?
1. Okoa	Yes	Yes	Yes	Yes	Yes
2. Ijagan	Yes	Yes	Yes	Yes	Yes
3. Odo-Owon	Yes	Yes	Yes	Yes	Yes
4. Ijalu	Yes	Yes	Yes	Yes	Yes
5. Isaba	Yes	Yes	Yes	Yes	Yes
6. Otun	Yes	Yes	Yes	Yes	Yes
7. Ahinke	Yes	Yes	Yes	Yes	Yes
8. Ilemla	No	No	Yes	Yes	No
9. Ido Egbe	No	No	Yes	Yes	No
10. Iloko	No	No	Yes	Yes	No
11. Opada	No	No	Yes	Yes	No

(Source: Egbe Chiefs, Representation Document, 1984)

Table 5 shows the traditional set up of the main chieftaincy titles especially in respect of Owa. It reveals that six out of the eleven clans are from Ile-Egbe while five clans come from Oke-Egbe, referred to as Egbe North and Egbe South respectively. The Table also shows that the position of Owa would have to rotate six times within Egbe North before moving to Egbe South once. It is this type of traditional realities that some people with an eye for political participation regard as unacceptable in the vibrant and modern Egbe. It may be useful to explain that 'Ahinke', strictly speaking, refers to three 'Akus', namely: Okedisin, Apoto and Ogba Onimosi (refer to Chapter 1). In loose usage, which is very common nowadays, it refers to all the 'Akus' at Oke-Egbe. Table 6 documents traditional titles, their origins and the nearest descriptions of their roles and functions.

Chapter 4: Chieftaincy Institutions

Table 6: Traditional Titles, Origins and Functions

No.	Titles	Origin	Nearest description of roles and functions
1	Owa	Ilesha	Traditional ruler
2	Asalu	Old Oyo	Deputy to Owa
3	Odunro	Old Oyo	Assistant to ruler
4	Alaofin	Old Oyo	Chief in charge of lands
5	Olu Agba	Old Oyo	Assistant to ruler
6	Olu Kekere	Old Oyo	Second Assistant to ruler
7	Ajagun	Old Oyo	General in the army
8	Ologun Agba	Old Oyo	Major-General in the army
9	Ologun Omode	Old Oyo	Brigadier-General in the army
10	Iroja	Old Oyo	Colonel in the army
11	Elu (a woman)	Old Oyo	Chief in charge of women affairs
12	Ogbomoya	Old Oyo; restricted to Okoa Kati, Ijagan, Ijalu, Odo-Owon, Isaba and Otun	Next to Elu and in charge of marriages; authorises Chieftaincy for women upon consultation with Elu, her boss
13	Odofin	Head of Ido Egbe	Channel of communication
14	Oba Opada	Political	Administrator for Opada clan
15	Aro (Oba Iloko)	Iloko	Head of Compound
16	Oju or Ojuina	Old Oyo	Master of Ceremony in the annual festivals
17	Ajagbonna	Old Oyo restricted to Okaofin	Head of Compound
18	Agbana	Old Oyo restricted to Apoto	The name of the priest of the god of 'Abidosi', 'Olobi Korogbo'. There is a rock at the site symbolising the god. The priest was not recognised as a chief but he later became accepted as the head of Compound
19	Ejio	Old Oyo	In charge of aliens; this is a title for a non-indigene given in recognition of her/his contributions to Egbe's development
20	Aduta (a woman chief)	Old Oyo	Restricted to all the six clans of Egbe North and also Okedisin and Etiyara
21	Olore Agba	Old Oyo	Priestesses of the goddess of fertility
22	Olore Kekere	Old Oyo	Co-priestesses of the goddess of fertility
23	Onikota (Ikota)	Old Oyo; formerly restricted to Okoa, Isaba	They report unusual appearances in town and offer sacrifices to the gods

		and Ainke but presently available in all clans as a result of integration – marriage and migration to live with other clans	as required; they do not normally act unilaterally as they are often directed by the Council of chiefs
24	Arainke	Restricted to Egbe South (Ainke)	Whenever power seemed concentrated in Egbe North (Ile-Egbe) the title is used to summon opposition or request a common action to such a power be it political, judicial or otherwise

As can be seen in Table 6, the first twelve traditional chiefs are listed according to the order of their seniority. Owa occupied the first position followed by Asalu, Odunro, Alaofin, etc in that order. Thus, Ajagun was the 7th chief in seniority while Iroja occupied the 10th position in rank. Elu occupied the 11th position assisted by her deputy, Ogbomoya, who occupied the 12th position. Both of them were in charge of women affairs and marriages.

It must be mentioned that today things are changing and they are different from past practices. The traditional chiefs do not appear to be as recognised and respected as they used to be. Readers can easily suggest a number of reasons for this state of affairs. In addition, modern chieftaincy institutions have also been in place to perform most of the roles hitherto performed by a variety of the traditional rulers. At Egbe we now have the Elegbe of Egbe, the overall head of all the chiefs in the town seconded by the Baale, normally regarded as his deputy. However, it is not automatic that the Baale will succeed the Elegbe, neither is it necessary to become a Baale first before being appointed an Elegbe. For example, Oba Denki was never a Baale before he was appointed the Elegbe. However, Oba Olokundu was a Baale first before he became the Elegbe. Readers can easily suggest some advantages and disadvantages for being a Baale before assuming the status of an Elegbe.

These individuals are responsible for running the affairs of the town. In practice, if the ruling Elegbe comes from Ile-Egbe, the Baale will have to come from Oke-Egbe and vice versa. The Governor of the State and by extension, the government of the day, all recognise the existence and role of these rulers in the administration of the town. Therefore, the Government pays traditional rulers and chiefs some allowances for their valued functions in maintaining stability and progress in their respective areas. Given the fact that there are currently two approved Third-Class chiefs at Egbe, (Baale of Egbe and Oba of Loko) one is not sure whether there are or there will be any seniority between current Third-Class chiefs at Egbe or among possible future Third-Class chiefs in the town. One still feels that the Baale is traditionally the deputy for the Elegbe but perhaps things need to be spelt out more clearly.

As indicated earlier, Kelae was the first Owa and he appointed other chiefs after due consultation with the clan heads. As Alaofin was the title with which he left Old Oyo, he gave the title to his younger brother and this title was initially restricted to Oke-Aofin in Egbe. As the town expanded, Alaofin was downgraded to be the fourth in hierarchy of Egbe chiefs so that the two brothers might not decide the affairs of the town without due consultations with other members of the ruling hierarchy.

The three main elders of Egbe town were selected from Okoa, Isaba and Ahinke. The leader of Egbe community was always chosen from Okoa and called Baba Egbe, the most senior and head of Ikota. The current one is JK Ogungbemi (Okoa) – Olori Egbe, the traditional Title Sharers. Ikotas are said to be the owners of Egbe Community and they are in charge of important occurrences such as invading armies or impending tragedies. Against such events they often appease the gods with sacrifices and organise defence forces. They also distribute Chieftaincy titles. Owa is the head of the traditional chiefs while Ikota is the head of all developments in the town. They are said to be the owners of the town and are not just concerned with its administration. Agba Ikota is rotated amongst the 'Akus' in the following order: Okoa, Isaba/Ijagan, Ijalu, Otun, Odo-Owon and Okedisin (Ainke).

In the pre-colonial days the eleven clans, represented by their chiefs, assembled at the following places where major decisions involving, for example, development and judiciary, were taken.

1. Orun-Egbe – The Heart of Egbe or 'Eguru Odo' where the Chief's official palace is built (Ajewo).

2. Oja-Egbe – the god there was offered sacrifices at the main market.

3. Igbo-Ogun – the forest of the god of iron –owned by Apoto people.

4. Idi-Obatala (Obata) – the Obatala (Obata) shrine is situated at Okoa at Ogbaroko.

Nowadays the courts of law have replaced all the shrines and their former locations are left as historical relics. Some people suggest that there may still be a few adherents to these shrines, which were regarded almost as a religion, but the number of such people must be few today.

Decline in the Status of Owa

Owa was a victim of an alien Western culture. Owa was highly revered as a god and he was regarded as sacred and therefore not to be seen in public. He could only be contacted through Asalu, his deputy. Owa, by the traditional practice, went out only on an important occasion once a year. This was usually at the Egbe Annual Festival, held at Odun Egbe. The woman chief, Elu must not meet Owa for some unknown reasons. Therefore whenever Owa wanted to go out, he must advise Elu so that she would stay indoors. This was because whenever they met face-to-face, the two of them would die, according to the traditional belief. There was a similar practice that Ogbomoya should not be seen by the Owa and whenever she went out, she always informed Owa to stay indoors.

As the early missionaries were alien to Egbe's culture they unknowingly recognised Asalu as the paramount ruler. This was because Asalu was the person who was seen all the time. Similar experiences occurred with the early government officials who only saw Asalu and not the actual ruler, Owa. Quite logically the missionaries could not accept that the ruler was never seen. With time, therefore, every effort was made to reduce the importance of Owa even by some indigenes who knew that they could never have access to the traditional title. These people appear to have succeeded. This is because traditional structures appear to be crumbling and these are being replaced with new and more modern structures. There are certain rites associated with the installation of a new Owa, that potential modern aspirants may not be interested in. This rite is reported to be outdated and obsolete and many people will not subscribe to such a practice today.

Chieftaincy discussions

There was a meeting of seven representatives each from Egbe South (Ainke) and Egbe North (Ile-Egbe) which took place on 14th November, 1955. The councillors present included, Mr P.A. Agana, Mr S.A. Agbo, and Mr D.A. Oshagbemi. The meeting was called to discuss chieftaincy issues and it took place at Egbe Reading Room opposite the present Town Hall. Below is an extract from the discussions:

Mr Dawodu:
"What will be the position of 'Ijoyes' … shall we ignore the 'Ijoyes?' Do you think that it is advisable to recognise the Owa as the Oba in accordance with the traditional regulation of our ancestors?"

S.A. Agbo:
"The system of 'Ijoyes' is not practicable nowadays as this cannot corroborate with the regulations suggested for the proposed constitution. In the past the Owa was only recognised by name as the Head of town but not in the real sense of a ruler."

P.A. Agana:
"Let us do away with the 'Ijoyes', they are out of date."

Jonah Arowosegbe:
"It is not true that Owa was merely recognised by name and not as a ruler. The Owa in the old times was the ruler and the authority recognised in Egbe. His assistant was Asalu. The law

of our tradition forbade Owa from attending public meetings. That was why his assistant, Asalu, was recognised by the first Resident to Egbe as the Oba since Owa failed to show himself to the Resident."

D.A. Oshagbemi:
"The position of 'Ijoyes' is not for the current Egbe."

The above extract illustrates the struggles between tradition and modernity at Egbe in the middle period of the 20th Century. However, both parties recognised the importance of the role of Owa. Nevertheless, the last Owa to rule Egbe executively was Owa Agbana (1931-1943). As suggested earlier one reason why advocates wanted to get rid of the institution of Owa was that they had no ancestral rights to the post of Owa but they would like to rule. Some people also believed that wealth can or should be able to buy chieftaincy titles! Funnily enough, some people would say, one honorary chief even advocated that his honorary title should be made permanent and hereditary! Others might regard this statement by the honorary chief as a serious business which is not funny at all. A third and perhaps the most important reason concerns the rituals involved. Many aspirants feel that these are outdated and should no longer be practised in today's world. There are others who would like to have the traditional system modernised and retained as it affords stability and continuity of desirable practices. It is also devoid of the bitterness inherent in the current modern system which suffers from instability.

It is to be noted that the rule of Egbe by the Nupes was imposed by the Colonial Administration only for administrative convenience as Egbe was never conquered by the Nupes. It was suggested that Asalu maintained a carefree attitude as he was recognised as the ruler in place of Owa Ashehinde, the actual ruler.

Writing about the history of Ibadan, Michael Crowder (1973) suggested that the Ekiti people together with Ijesha, Yagba and Akoko formed the Ekiti parapo or Ekiti confederation that ganged up against Ibadan. In 1886 Governor Maloney of Lagos sent Reverend Philips to the warring groups and after a meeting, the terms of peace were agreed. According to the terms of agreement members of the Ekiti confederation and Ibadan should be independent of each other. Although Egbe did not attend the Lagos conference, Yagba, represented by Egbe was accorded an independent status. In 1893, Captain Bowen, the first Resident of Ibadan, unilaterally divided Yagba land into three parts. This was because Egbe people refused to meet the Resident in order to demarcate their boundary. Captain Bowen was said to have summoned the ruler of Egbe at a point in time that he had the power to have fixed the boundary of Egbe at the ruler's house!

In the resulting partition Yagbaland was divided into three parts – Ilorin Province, Kabba Province and Ondo State. The descendants of Yagba people in Ondo State are still identified today by the Yagba dialect which they speak and they include settlers in places such as Irele, Ipao, and Aiyede. West Yagba was part of Ilorin province which was dominated by the Nupe in the Lafiagi-Pategi Division with its headquarters at Lafiagi. East Yagba people had their headquarters at Kabba town in Kabba Province.

It should be noted that Egbe was unique because it was surrounded by high and strong walls which provided a safe haven for up to sixty nine villages from many parts of Yagbaland, Bunnu, Kabba and Ekiti. The failure of the Nupe people to capture Egbe was in large measure due to the strong Egbe infantry who defended their city walls assiduously. Nevertheless, West Yagba with Egbe as the headquarters had Tsaba (also spelt as Siaba or Shaaba), a replica of Nupe rule, still established in Egbe. Therefore, in a bloody struggle, Yagba chiefs, acting together and headed by Egbe successfully agitated for the withdrawal of the Nupe rule. Following Egbe's defeat of the Nupes, Egbe was made the head of West Yagba District in 1930. This arrangement replaced the rule of Nupe District head (Etsu Pategi). Egbe thereafter continued to manage its own affairs as well as the affairs of the people of Yagbaland.

The last Tsaba to rule in Egbe hailed from Apoto. When Oba Owojaiye died in 1955 this Tsaba was not allowed to rule Egbe because he was illiterate and was not accepted as a full indigene. Hitherto, the two titles Oba and Tsaba had always come from the different sections of Egbe in part to ensure stability in the administration of the town. The emergence of Oba Babalola Denki was the result of a search for an educated successor to Oba Owojaiye. The appointment of Chief Denki reinforced the practice that one needs not be a Baale or Tsaba before being enthroned as the paramount Egbe Chief.

Oba Denki was regarded as a community head for Egbe town and not as a district head. Consequently, he was not graded by the Government of the day. Similarly, when Oba Olokundu was appointed the Elegbe of Egbe, he was not graded. However, the Chief fought for recognition and was able to bring back the Staff of Office, which Egbe was said to have lost since 1926, as he was subsequently graded a Second-Class Chief. One of the reasons why Chief Denki was not graded was the explanation that there was supposed to be only one graded chief in the whole of West Yagba and that Chief Mark Dada was already graded as the Olu of Okeri. In essence, there was no vacancy for another graded chief in the whole of West Yagba at that time!

The two posts, Elegbe and Baale, were created in 1955 when Oba Denki was appointed as the Elegbe and Oba Olokundu was made the Baale. This decision was made at a meeting of community elites on 14th November 1955 where a resolution to have both posts to run concurrently was made. As indicated earlier, to enhance some balance in the community affairs the two stools could not at the same time reside in the same section namely, Odo-Egbe and Oke-Egbe. Currently, however, the actions of some elites have been said to contribute to the problems of Egbe as these elites attempt to bypass the traditions of the people and impose new rules. For example, it is said that some elites who would like to rule have abandoned traditional rights while the traditionalists appear oppressed and this is a concern for future stability.

Tommie Titcombe and Egbe Politics\Traditions

When Tommie Titcombe came to Egbe in 1908, he was well received by Chief Asalu, Owa's deputy. Titcombe could not meet with the traditional ruler, Owa who was regarded as next to God! At a time when Agbana became the paramount ruler of Egbe he too acquired the highest traditional title of Owa until he was conspired against and dethroned. It was this dethronement that brought the title of Owa as the paramount traditional ruler to an end. Tommie Titcombe later returned to Canada in 1930 due to ill-health. He, however, came back to Egbe on two other visits before May 1968 when he died in Toronto, Canada.

Tommie Titcombe had tremendous influence on the politics of Egbe and Yagba as a whole. As indicated earlier, on arrival he was the guest of Asalu as Owa would not go into public places except at the Annual Egbe Festival (Odun Egbe).

It should be noted that slavery was already abolished when Titcombe arrived in Nigeria in 1908. It would be recalled that Egbe was protected with strong walls and able soldiers and this defence attracted migrants from neighbouring towns and villages who took refuge in Egbe. Tommie Titcombe had influence with the Colonial Administrator (Resident), but he was at loggerhead with the Asalu who would not embrace Christianity. Asalu wanted to dictate Titcombe's itinerary but Tommie Titcombe did not allow that to happen. The deposition of Oba Asalu was precipitated by an accusation by some people that dissident elements in the town had destroyed some trees.

Tommie Titcombe wrote:

"I told him (British Resident) the matter concerned a few trees, not belonging to anyone in particular, he said, 'well, is that all?'...."

When the Resident went to Ere, a town part way to Egbe, I called Chief Asalu to meet him there and because of Asalu's evil practices through the years, I banished him and his wives to Okoloke, where he died (Sophie de la Haye, 1995, p.41). During the trials of Oba Asalu, Chief Ampitan Agbana was in alliance with Tommie Titcombe and as a High Priest of the god 'Abidosi' he claimed conversion to Christianity. He changed his name to Paul Ampitan Agbana to register his Christian conversion. At this time Owa of Egbe was in residence at Isaba. Tommie Titcombe and Paul Ampitan Agbana were in secret alliance and Agbana's appointment as the Chief in place of Asalu was influenced by Titcombe.

Titcombe further commented:

"The new Chief Agbana, frequently visited me, and as soon as the church was finished he came to every service and sat with his people, listening to the words of God. Previously, the people were afraid of Chief Asalu. Now, with Chief Agbana attending, they had nothing to fear." (Sophie de la Haye, 1995, p.42)

"On December 31, 1913, some 800 believers met in Egbe church for a watch-night service. After we dismissed, the Christians went down to Chief Agbana's compound and sang until morning." Ibid. p.65.

"We arrived in Egbe on New Year's Day, 1915, a red-letter day in Rowland Bingham's life. As we neared the town, the last few miles led up a gradual incline to pass into the circle of hills bordering the town. A group of boys came running to meet us; then men and women all neatly dressed. At the top of the hill a regular procession met us with music and greetings. In the midst of the crowd was our Christian Chief Agbana, in a hammock. He alighted to welcome us, and offered his hammock to Mr Bingham, who declined, feeling that the taking of any pre-eminent place would dishonour the Lord, whose wonderful work of grace he was beholding." Ibid. p.70.

Baba Toba, who was a contemporary of Owa, Asalu and Paul Ampitan Agbana narrated the story to one of the authors. Baba Toba reported that Owa continued to rule but that this was unknown to Tommie Titcombe and the Colonial Administrator. Owa Ashehinde ruled for over 38 years as the longest reigning Oba in Egbe history and died on January 18, 1929. Unfortunately, Oba Paul Ampitan, the Agbana of Apoto, only ruled for about a year and died on December 28, 1929 (Olokundu, 1968). It should be noted that Tommie Titcombe did not recognise the existence of Owa Ashehinde because he could not meet him. Here, Tommie's alien culture was in conflict with Egbe tradition and culture. Paul Agbana was, of course, well aware of Egbe's culture and Tommie Titcombe recommended his approval as the Chief to the Colonial Administrator, Mr Cole. It was reported that the Resident came to meet the Owa, but the Owa failed to turn up. The Resident then authorised the Staff of Office to be withdrawn. Paul Agbana encouraged the Staff to be taken away stating:

"Give them their Staff, a stick, if anyone wants a stick he could get one at Gbogbo Stream".

Perhaps one should state that although Egbe was given a Staff of Office before the year 1919, the Ilorin Provincial Gazetteer gave, in that year, the following list of emirs, chiefs or political heads and their respective grade as reported by Phillip Lonsdale, a resident at Ilorin in the "Ilorin Annual Report-572/1919 No.89". The Resident reported that the following chiefs held Staffs of Office.

- Emir of Ilorin – 1st grade
- Emir of Pategi – 2nd grade
- Olupo of Ajasse-Ipo – 2nd grade
- Baro of Kabba – 3rd grade
- Oloffa of Offa – 4th grade
- Owa of Egbe – 4th grade

It was the Owa at Isaba who was given the Staff of Office. As indicated below the Staff of Office was subsequently lost.

Chief Paul Agbana had thought that the Staff would be given to him but this was not done and that was how Egbe was without a Staff of Office until 1989 when Oba J. O. Olokundu was accorded a Second-Class status. The coronation of the Chief was performed in 1993 – see Photograph 9. The fact was that Paul Ampitan, the Agbana of Apoto, did not come to power until 1928, ten years after the demise of Owa Ashehinde.

Egbe Chiefs
Oba Aina Owojaiye (1941-1955)

The appointment of Oba Aina Owojaiye marked another era of chieftaincy tussle between the supporters of the deposed Owa and the Agbana from Okedisin Ward. Some people were jailed and banished from Egbe. Oba Aina Owojaiye rose from the ranks of Ikota to be the Oba of Egbe and his ascendancy was supported by the missionaries. His grandmother was from Odo-Ere. He subsequently became the President of the court for West Yagba. Before the Oba died, a number of important institutions came into being. For example, Titcombe College was founded in 1951. Egbe Hospital was built in 1952 and Egbe Nurses Training (Midwifery) School was also founded in 1953.

In 1947 there was a general demand for Oba's Palace to be built for the Local Authority i.e. Chief of West Yagba. The then Northern Regional Government gave approval to Egbe's application for the Palace to be built in Egbe. The Oba, on one occasion when one of the authors was in attendance at a town meeting stated:

"You Egbe people should allow me to combine efforts to build the Palace. This is not a personal palace for me".

The Palace was built at a place called 'Orun Egbe' i.e. Egbe's Heart. It was a central place for Egbe at that time and chiefs, elders and citizens gathered there to take important decisions. Iyekolo (2006, p.17) described Oba Owojaiye as Aina Aganyin of Egbe and that the chief was a typical returnee from Ghana where he had exposure to Western civilization. Iyekolo also felt that it was this quality of his widespread interaction in another country, in addition to the chief's outstanding personality, that made his clan put him forward as the Oba of Egbe. Unfortunately, Oba Aina Owojaiye died in 1955.

Oba Joseph Babalola Denki (1956-1986)
Oba Denki was the first to assume the title Elegbe of Egbe when he became the ruler (sworn in on August 13, 1956). He was a devout Christian.

Political storms arose due to rivalry and chieftaincy disputes during his tenure of office. The Baale was also joined in the petitions, which started on January 3, 1967, with thirteen grievances. The allegations included financial mis-management, discontent with council rates, and several unauthorised and unaccounted for taxes and levies. Protest letters were sent to the District Officer and the West Yagba Native Authority. Egbe Development Community was formed and in a petition No.1 dated 24th February, 1967, grievances were levied against both the Elegbe and the Baale. On 15th March 1967 both the Elegbe and the Baale wrote to the District Officer to intervene.

On 1st December, 1968 the Elegbe of Egbe and Seven Council Members wrote to the Provincial Secretary at Lokoja, the Divisional Officer at Kabba and the Yagba N.A. Central Office at Isanlu. Their letter read in part:

"You will also be aware that the Provincial Secretary in Lokoja, Mr Aderibigbe, spent almost a week in Egbe and gave these people his fatherly advice, yet they kept an adamant ears to him. This prompted the Provincial Secretary to write a warning letter No. 524/54/211, dated 4th December, 1967 captioned 'uneasy calm in Egbe refers'." (Personal records of the authors)

The District and Divisional Officers Messrs Bello Mallam Katsina and Mallam Sanni had consistently participated in the issues raised. The Provincial auditor also had done his best and found no misappropriation or embezzlement of Council funds. Later on their public meetings were banned in the interest of peace in the town. The petitioners continued violent protests and even considered litigation at the magistrate court, Ilorin. In those days the Town Council had to declare for the ruling party in the Region i.e. the Northern Peoples Congress (NPC). There was no freedom of expression and action. The arms of Government, like the police, were used to suppress opponents and make them conform to the Government's views.

Several petitions were written against the ruler. A notable one was from a lecturer at Ahmadu Bello University on 1st November 1971. The petition was to get rid of Chief Denki and install someone else. The Administrator from Lokoja explained that Chief Denki could not be removed unless a majority substantiated the allegation of loss of confidence in him. Complaints about the illegal collection of funds by the government officials and misappropriation of the same could not be substantiated as the auditors always carefully checked all receipts.

A University lecturer complained of Chief Denki's tyrannical rule. The sole Administrator wondered how a Zaria-based lecturer could determine the oppression and tyranny of a ruler in Egbe. The Sole Administrator spent five days in Egbe and resolved that they should give peace a chance and appealed for co-operation for Egbe's development. One of the authors of this book, with others in the Development Committee and Egbe Community, jointly wrote a letter of appreciation to the Sole Administrator for his effort at resolving the disputes in the town. It appeared that too much time was spent on resolving disputes rather than on improving the development of the community.

Despite all the distractions Chief Denki's tenure of office was marked with remarkable developments. A local Government School was built in 1957 with a postal agency in 1959, which was upgraded to a modern Post Office in 1961. The Community built Egbe Girls School in 1968 and invited the Catholic Church to be the proprietor. The invitation of the Catholic Church instigated Titcombe College, a Protestant institution, to open its doors for girls to attend in what was previously an exclusively male Secondary School. There was the Egbe Water Project, which started in 1969 and was commissioned in 1975 by Bartlett, a Canadian missionary. Egbe Airfield and Town Hall were also built. All these show evidence of the efforts made to develop in a strife-torn society yearning for progress.

The Elegbe of Egbe, Chief Denki, died in 1986 after collapsing with a heart attack in Church. He was not known to have been graded as a chief by the Government of the day. Only Olu Okeri was graded as a Second-Class Chief and he was the Chairman of the Council of Chiefs for the whole of West Yagba during this period. Other chiefs were more or less regarded as village heads. When J B Denki ascended to the throne he was titled Elegbe of Egbe signifying the paramount ruler in Egbeland and signifying the oneness in the two sections of the town. He was therefore the first Elegbe of Egbe, a title which was regarded as perhaps more modern and embracing of the whole of Egbe. It should be pointed out that 'Oba' is a generic chieftaincy title while the Elegbe is a specific ruler of Egbeland.

Oba James Oluremilekun Adegboyega Olokundu (1987-1990)
Oba Olokundu was born into the family of Pa-Joseph Babalola Olokundu of Kati, sub clan of Okoa, Egbe in 1923. He had his primary education at St. Mathias Catholic School, Lagos. He then proceeded to Christ High School Lagos where he finished in 1939. He worked at the Marine department in Lagos untill 1942 and later in 1943, he enlisted into the Army. For two and a half years he worked in the Signal Corp in Burma during World War II. He was discharged on May 31, 1946 when he returned to Lagos as a Circulation Manager at Amalgamated Press Limited, Publishers of the Express Group of Newspapers.

He passed his examination in Industrial Accounts and took up a job as an accountant with the Church Missionary Society, Broad Street, now known as Murtala Mohammed Road, Lagos. On the invitation of his people, he came to Egbe in 1956 and was installed as the Baale of Egbe, a post which is second in rank only to the Elegbe of Egbe. Olokundu was informed of his appointment as the Elegbe of Egbe by a letter from the Secretary for the Oyi Traditional Council dated 18th January 1987. His tenure took effect from this date.

The perennial chieftaincy dispute in Egbe reared its ugly head again when some people from Oke-Egbe appointed O. A. Awe as the person to succeed the late Oba Denki who had passed away.

In a dramatic move a Chief in Egbe using television, radio and newspapers called a press conference. This was held in Ilorin where he reiterated the constitutional provisions to support his claim. These included (a) non-direct or automatic inheritance to the vacant stool of Elegbe, particularly with regard to Baale of Egbe, unless Kingmakers saw it fit to appoint him as Elegbe. (b) Oke-Egbe and Ile-Egbe should have equal representation totalling forty members with twenty seven forming a quorum in the Kingmaker's Committee. On August 28, 1984, twenty eight members out of 40 were in attendance thus forming a quorum. The Chief said that the Oba elect was then unanimously elected. The Oba-elect was to succeed the late Oba J. B. Denki who reigned for thirty years. (Awoniyi, B., Kwara Weekly, September, 19-22, 1984).

In a counter reaction to the Chief's suggestions, the Kwara Weekly, September 26-29, 1984, reported that:

Nobody has yet occupied the vacant stool of the Oba of Egbe, the Egbe Kingmakers (Ikotas) have claimed. Refuting claims made by the Chief that an Elegbe of Egbe had been "elected" in the 1956 constitution of Egbe Community, the Ikotas said that those who presented themselves as Kingmakers were not in fact Kingmakers. The Ikotas claimed that the Electoral College Group had no basis in the history of King-making at Egbe and suggested that no Yoruba Oba could be elected in a plebiscite. They further suggested that:

"... the instrument of selection has not been presented to Egbe so that the Kingmakers can perform their official duty."

While accusing the Chief of attempting to sabotage the selection procedure, the Ikotas condemned him over his 'election' claims as established in the media. The Ikotas were not aware of a 1956 constitution. Egbe as an ancient Yoruba town had some traditions and history, which governed the King-making process amongst others. The Ikotas alleged that the Chief falsified the records in giving the number of 'Akus' (clans) as sixteen instead of eleven. The Ikotas argued that as custodians of the customs and traditions of Egbe people, they would not allow those who disrespect tradition to turn Egbe into a tradition-less community. (Kwara Weekly, September 26-29, 1984).

There were other exchanges of accusations and counter accusations between the Chief and the Kingmakers and some of these unfortunate allegations appeared in the Nigerian Herald Newspapers. The Chief held a press conference reported by the Nigerian Herald publication of 18th September, 1984 while the Ikotas (Kingmakers) discredited the press conference which they regarded as reckless and explosive. The Ikotas argued that it was Ile-Egbe's turn to elect the Oba of Egbe. They appealed to the Sole Administrator to initiate the selection process without delay and pledged their unflinching support to the State

Government. The clans represented were Okoa, Otun, Isaba, Ijagan, Ijalu and Odo-Owon and copies of their letters were sent to the following people amongst others:

- Chairman, Oyi Traditional Council of Chiefs
- Oyi Traditional Council of Chiefs
- Chief of West Yagba
- Baale of Egbe
- Traditional Chiefs – Egbe Community Branches, Lagos, Kaduna, Zaria

With the announcement of the approval of Oba Egbe's appointment of 17th January 1986 due to take effect on 18th January 1986 and the Oba's installation scheduled for March 2, 1986, the dispute took a new turn. The opposing side reacted by taking court action with 'Application of a Writ of Summons' in the High Court of Kwara State, Ilorin, between Oba Adekunle Awe Olu, as the plaintiff (Isaba Ward, Ile-Egbe) and the following:

- Chief J. O. Olokundu, Baale of Egbe
- Mr Oye, Sole Administrator, Oyi-local government
- Oyi traditional council
- Attorney General, Kwara State, Ilorin as the defendants

The Application was dated 26th day of February 1986. Oba Adekunle Awe Olu's Solicitor was J. O. Ijaodola from Ilorin. The case was decided in favour of Chief J.O. Olokundu who was then made the Elegbe of Egbe. He ruled until his death in 1990.

Oba Stanley Kayode Owa (1990-)
The current Elegbe came into office in 1990 and he has been working towards the unity and the overall development of the town. As indicated earlier he faces many obstacles as a result of the lack of unity in the two constituent parts of the town. Progress is however being made in several areas and this is reflected in developments such as the facelift of the town and the recognition of the Elegbe of Egbe as a First-Class Chief for the first time in 2006. The government also approved two

additional chieftaincy positions for Egbe. These are third-class chieftaincy titles for the Baale of Egbe and the Oba of Loko.

The many problems of the town include the continual chieftaincy disputes which often degenerate to acrimony and hostility. A lot of money has been wasted in the courts of law as the traditional system of selection has been frequently challenged in court. Sometimes there have been problems of tradition conflicting with modernisation. Several people have spoken to us to express awareness of some of these problems. Some people are concerned for the future stability and progress of Egbe and for the survival of our traditional institutions. Avarice and dishonesty appeared to have robbed Egbe of its traditional values in the selection of chiefs.

From the historical analysis reviewed thus far, it appears that Egbe Chieftaincy disputes have become endemic. All Egbe citizens are therefore encouraged to find a way out of the many court cases that they tend to place themselves in. It is safe to conclude that the people look forward to a peaceful town with significant economic progress under the leadership of their new First-Class Chief, HRH, Oba Stanley Kayode Owa.

The Chief possesses a diploma in business administration, a bachelor's degree in political science and he is a retired major in the Nigerian army. He is a member of the Okun Traditional Council and Chairman of the West Yagba Traditional Council (Iyekolo, 2006, p. 137).

Table 7 shows the rulers of Egbe from about 1500 to 2008, the current year of writing. It shows Kelae as the first Owa of Egbe and that after him there were another thirty-eight Owas from a period of about 1500 to 1880 when a record was obtainable. Owa Ashehinde and Oba Asalu Fayomi were contemporaries.

Table 7: The Rulers of Egbe (about 1500 – 2006)

	Names	Title	Ward	Period
1	Owa Kelae	Owa	Okoa	}
2	38 Owas	Owa	Okoa	} about 1500-1880
3	Owa a do nina awere a patu	Owa	Okoa	}
4	Female Owa	Owa	Ijagan	}
5	Owa Ashehinde	Owa	Isaba	1894-1928
6	Oba Asalu Fayomi	Asalu	Okedisin	1894-1910
7	Oba Paul Ampitan	Agbana	Apoto	1928-1929
8	Owa Agbana	Owa	Okedisin	1931-1943
9	Oba Aina Owojaiye	Ikota	Ijalu	1943-1955
10	Oba Joseph Denki	Elegbe of Egbe	Apoto	1956-1982
11	Oba James Olokundu	Elegbe of Egbe	Okoa	1987-1990
12	Oba Stanley Owa	Elegbe of Egbe	Okedisin	1990-

A new political structure should emerge now because Egbe is indivisible and the rights of all should be protected under a single political administration. The community should begin to think of how to remove the fighting and acrimony that is often associated with the appointment of either the Baale or the Elegbe of Egbe. The authors are of the opinion that the court cases that often accompany the appointment of persons into these high offices debase the glamour and the respect of the offices.

Honorary Chiefs
During the reign of Oba J B Denki, the Elegbe of Egbe, honorary chiefs were appointed in recognition of their services to the community and or as patronage for loyalty. It was suggested that some people exerted pressure on the Elegbe for representation on the traditional Council. The Elegbe who hailed from Apoto, Ainke, told people that he had community leaders but not enough traditional chiefs there to compose a traditional Council. Consequently the Elegbe created several chieftaincy positions so that the majority of the Council of traditional chiefs would not have to come from Ile-Egbe. Table 8 documents some of these appointments.

Table 8: Egbe Non-Traditional Chiefs Appointed by the Elegbe of Egbe, Oba Denki

	Title	Title holder	Nearest description of post	Place of abode
1	Basorun	Chief O. Simoyan	Prime Minister	Oke-Egbe
2	Aare	Chief J. Owojaiye	Captain General	Ile-Egbe
3	Gbegbegun	Chief T. Arosanyin	Political Adviser	Oke-Egbe
4	Ajiroba	Chief O. Dada	Councillor General	Oke-Egbe
5	Bobajoko	Chief Monselu Oju	Ward Leader	Ile-Egbe
6	Gbobato	Pa Ogunjobi	Chief Supporter	Oke-Egbe
7	Kabobaro	Bolaji Agbana	Chief Supporter	Oke-Egbe
8	Gbobaro	Alaya Gbanko	Chief Supporter	Oke-Egbe
9-14	Gbobaro	Six other chiefs	Chief Supporter	Oke-Egbe
15	Bobajiro	Chief David Ajayi	Adviser	Oke-Egbe
16	Tobase	Chief Tommy Aremu	Supporter	Oke-Egbe

However, some people felt that the appointment of the non-traditional chiefs was reminiscent of the obsolete 'Arainke' title created to offset the concentration of traditional chiefs in Ile-Egbe. Of the sixteen honorary chieftaincy titles, therefore, only two were from Ile-Egbe and fourteen were from Oke-Egbe. It was alleged that in this instance it was the concentration of traditional chiefs in Ile-Egbe that caused the creation of new honorary titles with the majority of them at Oke-Egbe. The spirit behind the new appointment of the non-traditional chiefs was to provide or create a number of chieftaincy positions that would be numerically nearer if not greater than the ones that exist at Ile-Egbe.

Voices were raised against the award of honorary chieftaincy titles in Egbe. In a letter dated 8th July, 1981 to the then Elegbe of Egbe, Oba Denki, Chief Owojaiye stated that while he agrees that the Oba of Egbe has the right to award honorary titles to people, he felt that such a decision was always held in trust for the people of Egbe. In addition, he suggested that the traditional principle of Chief and Council appeared to have operated with an invisible Council on that occasion. He also suggested that the majority of Egbe people were opposed to the award of chieftaincy titles at that period in time for a number of reasons among which are:

(a) that the ten titles awarded the previous month were sufficient for the time being, and more importantly,

(b) that all those that were awarded titles on 31st July 1981 belong to a particular political party and he reasoned that our chief must not be seen to be partisan (Owojaiye, J. A., 1981, pp.1-2).

Thus, there were criticisms of the composition of the chieftaincy titles as the overwhelming majority of them have come from only one section of Egbe community and also appeared to have come from a particular political party of the day. Yet, traditional chiefs are not expected to play partisan politics on matters of societal development in Egbe.

The competition for development ought not to cause friction and hatred. Unity within Egbe will lead to unity with her neighbours. There are times when the internal feud is submerged to face a common problem. For instance in a demand for the Headquarters of West Yagba to be sited in Egbe, the people who petitioned did so on behalf of Egbemekun. Egbe Community argued that Egbe was accessible to all other villages in the district as well as the other parts of the State.

In 1947 when there was a general demand for Oba's Palace for the Local Authority Chief for West Yagba the then Northern region Government gave approval to Egbe's application for the palace to be built at Egbe. At that time it was made clear to the neighbouring nine villages that there could only be one Oba's palace for West Yagba and that Egbe had been authorised to build the palace that would serve all purposes. Unfortunately, the building stands there today without anybody occupying it. Egbe Community ought to cooperate, renovate and modernise the palace to be used by the Oba of Egbe i.e. the Elegbe of Egbe. This may assist in the solution of some of the problems of unity in the town. A palace is a community building for community use.

Many suggestions continue to be offered by Egbe indigenes to solve these problems and conflicts. These suggestions include the creation of (honorary) non-traditional chiefs and that traditional chiefs should be called Egbe Mekun chiefs. There is also the suggestion for the creation of Egbe community chiefs. The latter group of chiefs would emanate from people who were not born in Egbe but who have contributed to the development of the community and the Elegbe of Egbe feels that it is appropriate to honour them. Our concern here is to make an open invitation to all the people from neighbouring towns and villages that are not indigenous sons and daughters of Egbe but who wish to settle and live in Egbe to do so. They are all invited also to participate in the affairs of Egbe in a transparent and open fashion without any discrimination.

The old official Oba's palace (Ajewo) is depicted in Photograph 8. Oba Olokundu and members of his family actually lived in the Palace for a long time before they moved to live in their modern personal residence. All other Egbe chiefs, including the current one, have lived in their personal residences. Petty traders sometimes utilised the vast land area of the old Palace to display their wares. The Coronation of His Royal Highness, the Elegbe of Egbe, Chief Olokundu in 1993 is shown in Photograph 9. Here, the Chief is receiving his staff of office as a Second-Class Oba from Governor Abubakar Audu, the State Governor at the time.

Chapter 4: Chieftaincy Institutions

Photograph 8: Old Official Oba's Palace (Ajewo)

Photograph 9: The Coronation of Elegbe of Egbe – Chief Olokundu

Chapter 5: The Legacy of the Early Missionaries

There are three important legacies left by the early missionaries for the people of Egbe. These are mainly in the areas of education, health-care provision and religion. This chapter discusses, in the main, the educational legacies. Other writers are encouraged to explore the two other legacies in a more detailed way. This would give an informed and rounded discussion of the overall legacies bequeathed by the missionaries. A discussion of the current challenges faced by the town will also be helpful as well as suggestions offered for the future.

The Sudan Interior Mission, SIM, was the organisational medium through which several missionaries from Canada, the USA and England came to Egbe. This chapter reviews the early educational development at Egbe and points out that this is associated with the primary objective of evangelisation by the missionaries. It discusses the origin of Titcombe College and documents the names and roles of each of the principals from inception until the present time. It also reiterates the role of the teaching and non-teaching staff members and suggests that the College has had a cordial relationship with the Egbe community. Only brief comments are made about Egbe hospital and the impact of Christian religion on the lives of the people.

Early Educational Development

It is to the eternal credit of the early missionaries, especially Tommy Titcombe, that Western education was established in Egbe. Following the introduction of the educational institutions was the establishment of medical facilities in the town. The story of the SIM began on 4th December 1893 with three pioneering missionaries, namely: Walter Gowans, Thomas Kent and Rowland Bingham. Their aim was to establish an African Industrial Mission, but the name was later changed to the Sudan Interior Mission which comprised Christian missionaries from different denominations such as Methodist, Baptist, Anglican, and other protestant denominations.

Both Gowans and Kent went into the hinterland and established stations at Bida and Pategi. At the end of 1894 the two men died and Bingham, who was left alone in Lagos to communicate with the outside world, went back to Canada in frustration. In 1898, Bingham formed a Christian Council for the Sudan at Toronto (Kalu O. 1978, p.40) and thus the mantle of leadership fell on Bingham alone. In 1900 he returned to Nigeria with two other colleagues. On arrival at Lagos he was sick and was sent back home to recuperate. His companions also went back. However the 'unknown' Sudan had germinated in the short time that the three missionaries from Canada had come to Nigeria.

On his return to Nigeria, Reverend Bingham, who lived to organise one of the largest Christian Missions in the world, decided upon an international interdenominational initiative. Defending this action he stated:

"In whatever ecclesiastical party one finds himself placed, he is blind who does not recognise that outside it are some of the best Saints that God and grace have made, and to whom every yearning of Christian love draws one..."
(Bingham in Oshatoba, 1985, p.8)

In 1903, Bingham sought permission to open some Christian centres. Permission was granted and some Christian stations were opened at Bida and Pategi where, expansion of SIM schools became feasible because there were independent non-Moslem tribes (Graham, 1966). In this category was Yagba. In 1906 Reverend David Osainnaiye Adeniyi invited Nakoju, who came from Pategi, to join him in a visit to Oba Egbe where they were both happily received and continued in their Missionary Witness. Tommy Titcombe arrived in Nigeria in September 1908 and was introduced to a companion, David Osainnaiye Adeniyi from Ogga. They both travelled several days by narrow bush path from Pategi to Egbe in November 1908 to begin missionary activities among the Yagba people.

Many people were eager to receive the missionaries and it was decided that Egbe should be the headquarters of their activities. Consequently, from that day Tommy Titcombe has

Chapter 5: The Legacy of the Early Missionaries

been called 'Oyinbo Egbe', the White man of Egbe. Egbe also became the headquarters for SIM in Southern Nigeria and a centre for Christian activities where missionaries were trained for field work. In 1909, SIM activities extended to Mopa, Ponyan and all towns and villages along the road. In August 1911 Guy Plafair arrived in Egbe and in 1912 he left Egbe to open a new station at Oro-Ago in Igbominaland. Missionary activities later extended to Minna, Miango, Kagoro and Kaltungo. It appeared that Lord Lugard fell out with the SIM over religious doctrine. He was reported to have stated:

"I am informed that they preach the equality of Europeans and natives, which, from a doctrinal point of view, is apt to be misapplied by people in a low stage of development... and interpreted as abolition of class distinction..." (Fafunwa, 1980, p.2).

While Western Education was introduced by Tommy Titcombe, this was done alongside indigenous education. The purpose was to train the staff needed by the missionaries such as cooks and evangelists. While the missionaries learnt the local language in order to communicate with the natives, at the same time the indigenous people were taught the English language. Egbe became the centre where the Yoruba language and other languages were taught. After such teaching, people were dispersed to the outlying villages/ stations following a three months' orientation programme. Missionaries were expected to pass an examination in language proficiency. Many of them found it difficult to learn as the local languages and dialects are tonal and the structure is quite different from European languages. Nigerian vernaculars vary substantially even from one village to the next. Any one missionary had to learn a number of dialects and that is why some missionaries stayed for a long time in just one station.

The earliest primary school was located in the missionary compound and pupils were also trained as interpreters. There were codes of conduct solely for the white missionaries on their relationship with the blacks who were regarded as heathens. The missionaries were presumed to have a superior culture and nothing in the African culture was regarded as good enough. The morality of kinship ties in the supportive extended African family system and African art were ignored. To them, Africans had a monopoly of superstition of African ancestors and secret societies. One of the authors was informed by his mother that the sculpture representing his twin sister was taken away by one of the early missionaries to a European country as a pretext of breaking the family from image worshipping.

There were, of course, some social evils that the missionaries had to confront. Such practices include the degradation of women, child marriage, widowhood, defective family training, slavery, witchcraft, neglect of the poor and the sick, cruelty, poor sanitary conditions, superstition and the practice of keeping concubines. Many slaves were freed in Egbe due to the intervention of Tommy Titcombe. The intervention of the missionaries appeared to have broken the solidarity of the indigenous culture in Egbe. In Chinua Achebe's words:

"The white man is very clever... now he has won our brothers, and our clan can no longer act as one. He has put a knife on the things that held us together and we have fallen apart" (Achebe, 1994, p.176).

Sunday school classrooms and church premises were used to teach Western education. The objective was to train converts who would become Christian leaders and some missionaries were criticized for compromising too much with the local people. Bible School teachings started in Egbe in 1914 and later in 1928 moved to Agunjin until its movement in 1930 to the current place at the Theological Seminary, Igbaja. The College currently awards degrees up to the doctoral level in Theology. As a development the Evangelical Church of West Africa (ECWA) Theological College, Oyi, was opened in 2001 and the first Principal was Rev. M.T. Babaleke from Egbe.

Formal primary school education started in 1909. The early missionaries introduced the curricular to meet the vocational requirements of the period and they trained catechists, teachers, interpreters, cooks and other mission workers needed. Emphasis was placed on reading, writing, religion and arithmetic. The primary school, which was localised at Egbe, became centralised in 1925 while it served Yagba and Igbomina districts. In 1936 the first pupils from this centralised school system received their First School Leaving Certificate in an examination conducted by the Government in Lokoja. Mrs C.P. Jensen Adetutu was the principal of the School. In 1933 there was agitation for more English lessons and this was granted in 1935. The policy, which was initially colonial, was gradually blending old ways with the new ones without resulting in many problems.

Initially, SIM schools seemed to have interpreted their educational policy too rigidly. Pupils and converts were forbidden from using western clothes such as skirts, trousers, gowns and shoes. This policy was, however, overturned in the 1950s by the new brand of young dedicated missionaries. Many of them were well qualified theologians, medical doctors, engineers and educationalists of no mean calibre. Their mission was to prepare the youths of the country for a changing industrial and civilized world. Secondary schools, hospitals and health training institutes were built. Though the SIM was a pioneer of educational institutions in Egbe, other denominations such as the Salvation Army (1926) and the Catholic Church (1968) arrived at the scone and contributed to the overall educational development at Egbe.

The Origin of Titcombe College
Titcombe College, named after its progenitor, Tommy Titcombe, is situated south west of the town near Egbe Hospital. It was opened on the 26th January, 1951 at a temporary site where the present 1st ECWA Church is located. As a participant, one of the authors recounted that the first set of students were thirty in number and that they were of different ages ranging from twelve to nineteen. The time spent in the Church was brief and the class was moved in March 1951 to its permanent site which is opposite the ECWA Hospital. The area of land occupied by the College was about twenty acres. Initially, only two rooms were built with grass thatched roof. One was a classroom while the other was a store and the Principal's Office. From the beginning the students were multi-ethnic comprising Yorubas of different

sub-tribes and Ibo. Later admissions included the Hausas, Fulanis and a student from Niger Republic. The College is named after the first Canadian Christian missionary, who arrived in Egbe in November 1908, Tommy Titcombe. Emphasis was placed on Christian teachings and qualitative secular subjects as well as the sciences. The SIM as the proprietor had well qualified teachers and modern science equipment was brought to the college. At its height, Titcombe College was probably one of the best colleges in Nigeria. Even the renowned University of Ibadan had to borrow some of the science laboratory equipment of the College for their own use. Sometimes the College owned more equipment than was needed. In such cases the extras were sold to ready buyers.

Titcombe College very early emphasised spiritual matters, not only in its curriculum but also in its mode of life and activities. Bicycles were bought for evangelism into the surrounding villages in Yagba. The staff members went with students on their vehicles to preach in the local churches around Egbe and the surrounding villages. The emphasis in scholarship was on the sciences which marked Titcombe College as a great college. In addition there was adequate provision for sporting and recreational activities. The motto of the college was 'Learn and Worship' and this motto is reflected in the distinguished performances of the College. The education offered was a well-rounded one. Most of the building structures were built with the co-operation of the staff and the students. Students were taught how to wire houses and most of the school building and wiring work was done with the assistance of the students. Before dormitories were built, students had to walk from their respective houses in the town through the bushes and narrow paths to the college at about 7am in order not to be late for the assembly at 7.30am. During the forty-five minutes break for lunch, students cooked or prepared their meals while others brought 'gari' or other prepared meals from home. It was from such humble beginnings that the renowned Titcombe College developed.

Up until the early 1980s the college had well equipped mechanic and carpentry workshops, a photographic studio, standard performing arts and a literary club. It also had an appropriately staffed and stocked medical centre. Other facilities included five standard football fields – one of which is complete with good athletics facilities for track and field events. There was also four courts each for lawn tennis and basketball; one modern swimming pool and a standard indoor sports centre that housed several games such as table tennis, billiard, snooker, chess, 'ayo', etc. Virtually all dormitories had their own table tennis facilities. Indeed, Titcombe College also had a well equipped sports store with requisite materials like jerseys, balls and soccer boots. Titcombe College never fell below the second position in sports and athletics competition in the then Northern Nigeria. The college science club produced a radio transmitter/receiver in 1965 and the College has produced many renowned professors and academics, serving in institutions of higher learning within and beyond the shores of Nigeria.

One of the best medical surgeons in Canada today is an Old Titcombe student. In the armed forces of Nigeria there are also Generals either serving or retired. For example, the immediate past Chief of the Naval Staff in Nigeria is an old T.C. student. A few old students have served in the diplomatic mission. In fact, the Organisation of African Unity Ambassador to the United Nations, an indigene of the Niger Republic, is an old student of Titcombe College.

The training of young Christians to be involved in gospel work, Christian fellowship activities and teaching in the Sunday Schools represent some of the Christian traditions of the college. On 24th March, 1970 there was a turning point in the tradition of the college as the visiting Commissioner for Education, Alhaji S S Amego, declared in the college auditorium that no student should thereafter be asked or forced to attend the church. Earlier, there had been an infiltration of non-Christian students into the College and these were mainly Moslems. The Sunday after Commissioner Amego's announcement was rowdy. There was an unprecedented student eruption and the first African principal was targeted. The last expatriate principal, Paul Haney remarked:

"...where do we go from here? This college is not going on as a Christian school. God has more in this school than getting a West African School Certificate." (Haney, 1970).

This episode might be regarded as the beginning of the tragic loss of the fundamental objectives of the school.

Since that time there have been continual disciplinary problems for the College. The situation became worse as in 1972 the State School Board took over the running of the School and this event precipitated the divided loyalty of the teaching staff. As the staff could not serve two masters effectively at the same time, they suffered conflict of roles. There was a lot of pressure to increase the number of students to be admitted with little or no consideration for any increase or improvement in the facilities to sustain such increases.

The population explosion of the college coupled with the economic misfortunes of the nation adversely affected the growth and development of the college. The laboratories and infrastructures deteriorated seriously and needed urgent repairs or outright replacements. As at the time of writing, Titcombe College lives in the shadows of its past glories.

The principals of Titcombe College

1. Dale Blumhagen opened the college on 26th January 1951 as an Acting Principal and his tenure of office ended on 31st December 1952. He was a retired Army Officer from the USA and both he and his wife were devoted Christians and conscientious workers. Dale taught all the subjects except health science which was taught by his wife, Margaret. Some sports like boxing were introduced and military drill was popular at that time. Sometimes the couple invited students to share meals with them at their house.

2. Harris Poole was in the post from January to November 1953 as the Acting Principal: He remained at the college after this time and presented the first group of students for the West African School Certificate examinations in 1956 when Howard Dowdell was away in Canada on furlough.

3. Howard Dowdell (1953-1956), was the first substantive principal from Canada, where he had obtained a BSc degree in Mechanical Engineering. He came from a family of internationally renowned scientists and it was almost

incredible for those who knew his background to agree that he would become a young Christian working in Africa.

Dowdell was a missionary with an immense capacity for hard work and honesty. He graduated from the University of Toronto, from Pairie Bible College and from Harvard University where he earned a doctor of education degree in psychometric evaluation. He was married to Marion a missionary originally from Boston, USA and a registered nurse in Egbe, and they are blessed with children who are today serving in various capacities as a medical doctor and computer scientist. He is now retired in Toronto, Canada, after being the executive director of the Canadian Centre for World Mission. The quality of education at Titcombe College was very high and the School maintained good relationships with the Egbe Community and sister institutions especially the University of Ibadan. Dowdell was interested in extending electricity into Egbe town and was concerned with the lack of good water supply for the College, Egbe hospital and the community.

At the beginning of its second-year of classes, thirty first-year boys and another thirty boys, then in the second year, were seated at simple desks in two classrooms finished with cement floors, whitewashed mud brick walls and grass roofs. Along one side of each classroom a covered veranda kept out the sun and rain. The walls along the black wooden shutters hinged outwards from the lintels. A library of similar size contained perhaps a thousand books, mostly gifts from Christian publishing houses. Aside from the rows of mandatory textbooks there was very little to stimulate science in young minds other than an obsolete World Book Encyclopaedia and a big dictionary. The laboratory was as long as two classrooms and had a thatched roof but no ceiling. There were two cupboards for chemicals and equipment, fifteen benches, thirty stools, a teacher's desk and a blackboard. There was no sink or water supply, no electrical service and no provision for gas for Bunsen burners. Illumination only came with the shutters propped open in the daytime. Aside from a supply of test tubes there was little glassware or equipment. Dale and Margaret Blumhagen and Rowena Marion had braved their way through the first year of studies '...with little or no budget and a great deal of faith and courage'. Harris Poole who arrived late in the first year to teach history, English, and Bible studies, helped with sports. Rowena, a veteran of World War II taught mathematics classes.

As indicated earlier, the first-year students were twelve to nineteen years in age and they were marginally competent in the English language. Motivation was never a problem because a high school diploma gave promise for a life away from the toil of farming in a harsh developing world. Dowdell said that he was delighted at the attitude of the boys but he was overwhelmed that they would face exams on a par with children in England where education had a background in the homes and in the rich conversation of the culture.

Dowdell further said that he was supposed to be a teacher but that he had never taught more than in Vacation Bible Schools to children whose English language was well developed. Consequently, he was challenged to make an educational experience happen for desperately eager children but with none of the familiar laboratory equipment or basic utilities available in Canada. He wondered where to start, what to say and how to communicate in clear, simple English and he stated that he silently prayed for God to provide guidance.

Dowdell reported that he began teaching general science by following the steps of the textbook but he discovered that the children had diligently memorised the words of the text, but with little comprehension of their meaning. He suggested that much of their background in elementary schools had featured rote memorising, somewhat like the Moslem children endlessly repeating unknown words and phrases from the Koran overseen by a stern Malam or teacher under a shady mango tree. While his students all wanted him to teach them the magic words of science so that they could pass exams, they had not considered that they had wonderful minds that could probe and examine and understand the things of science.

Gradually Dowdell learnt how to couch his words, how to open the minds of his students in a science demonstration and by watching their faces, to discover whether learning was actually happening. At a point he decided that the only way to release the students from their slavery to the memorising of text books was to collect all the text books, lock them up and teach the syllabus in down-to-earth demonstrations through individual experimental trials and in classroom discussion. The West African School Certificate examination results proved, to a large extent, that he was successful in this experiment. Dowdell later reported that he was delighted to find them enjoying science instead of just memorising impressive but meaningless words. He indicated that he enjoyed the company of the students and learnt how to cause learning to happen in maths, physics and chemistry.

When the school was in its third year, a delegation of students appealed to Dowdell to host a science club. He accepted the challenge although it meant that he would be working for about 18 hours daily. On their part the students sacrificed their precious after-school free time.

When Dowdell was asked to take on the leadership at Titcombe College as Principal, he reported that he was thrilled with the progress of the students in every phase of their development. He said that the teaching staff members were a strong team of great people and he felt that Titcombe College was becoming a model for many such schools in developing countries. He reported that in the third year of its establishment, the College was in a debt of over 3,480,000 pounds to the SIM Treasurer. The students needed dormitories, more equipment, improved library a good diet and medical help. There was guidance in spiritual matters and guidance to maintain the Christian traditions of the College with love for God and the neighbours.

As earlier indicated, on November 26 1954, Marion and Howard got married in Egbe Church in the presence of all the students and the district missionaries. Bill Crouch was the officiating minister and George Campion was the best man while Beth Webb was the bridesmaid. The reception was at George Campion's house and the honeymoon took place in Lokoja. The bride and groom were taken there by the mission aeroplane and they returned to Egbe through Oyi airport.

The relationship of the hospital and Titcombe College was very good and students were given preferential treatment as they had to visit the hospital at a certain time of the day. In 1957

Howard Dowdell was transferred to Jos to be the first Education Secretary for the SIM and to direct the education programme for West Africa. Dowdell believed in the acceleration of the promotion of indigenes to take up posts being held by the expatriates. He saw to the opening of more schools such as Kagoro Secondary School and Kwoi Girls' School. Dowdell co-ordinated the then Anglophone and Francophone mission educational institutions in the countries of West Africa. These were farm schools in Niger and elementary schools in Monrovia, Liberia, that served a variety of people. There were also Bible Schools in Niger, Belarus, and Bourkina Faso. Details of Howard's experiences can be found in his book (Dowdell, HF, 2002). James Dada, one of the authors of this book, was his houseboy from the time that Dowdell came to Titcombe College in 1952. Consequently Dada was often with Dowdell when the latter repaired mission vehicles at the hospital workshop.

4. Charles Frame (1957-1965) was a family man and promoted family community relationships. He also sustained the rapid physical development of the College (Old Students Association, 1996), 'Brief history of Titcombe College', pp.10-12.

5. Jim Kraakevik obtained a doctorate in physics and served from 1966 to 1971. He was a professor of physics at Wharton College in Illinois. Together with Howard, they decided on a short-term missionary program by which teachers could be employed on a two-year term strategy. R. J. Davis, General Director, approved the programme. Thus, SIM short-term missions were born.

6. Paul Haney (1967 – 1970) was a chemistry teacher as well as the master in charge of sports. He was also in charge of gospel activities. During his tenure the College purchased over 50 bicycles for gospel evangelistic campaigns into villages around Egbe. He also taught the maintenance of these bicycles.

7. Justus Olu (1970-1974) was the first African principal of the College. It was suggested that the SIM in Jos wanted Mr S. Sayomi and he was accordingly transferred to Titcombe College. There, however, he met the Vice Principal, Justus, who was favoured by the local community to be the Principal. The Board of Education met and decided on the appointment of Justus Olu with the support of the State Government through the Area Inspector of Secondary Schools. Unfortunately, the situation provoked ethnic rivalry and an attack was organised against the incumbent with complaints about poor food. Justus was a well disciplined principal and he was meticulous in financial matters. He lodged a large sum of money into the College account and maintained the academic discipline of the school.

8. Babalola Olaoba (1974-1975) was of the Anglican denomination. He was transferred from Bishop Crowther Memorial Secondary School, Lokoja, to Titcombe College, Egbe.

9. Job Adewunmi (TC No. 199) 1976 to 1980, was the first old student of the College to head the institution. He completed his secondary education at the College in 1961. Adewunmi later became a chemistry teacher and loved the school, the staff and the students. His excellent relationships cut across age, ethnic loyalty and cultural barriers. He was an effective leader and a devoted principal. His life at Titcombe College was similar to that of Howard Dowdell in one important aspect. Each of them attracted government funding and support to the College. The director of education for the North accidentally visited Titcombe College and subsequently awarded a grant when Dowdell was the principal. This also happened when George Agbazika Innih, the then Military Governor of Kwara State, awarded grants to the College when Adewunmi was the principal. George came from his home town in Bendel State (now Edo State) on that memorable Sunday afternoon and called at Titcombe College where he met Job Adewunmi inspecting the students' food in the dining hall. It was at that point that Job

won the heart of George and he awarded unprecedented government grants and recognition as well as a giant bus to Titcombe College.

10. David Yeye-Odu (TC No. 152), 1981-1993 is an indigene from Egbe. He became the principal in an era that witnessed a population explosion in the College and this was associated with inadequate facilities and infrastructures. The standard of education unfortunately fell during his tenure and has not fully recovered, even to the present day. Yeye-Odu, otherwise known as 'moderate', was the longest serving principal of the college as he was the head for about thirteen years. The failures experienced during his tenure of office were associated with the downturn of the economic fortunes of the nation. Unfortunately, the existing facilities of the College such as louvers, beds, and doors were vandalised or stolen. The giant generator that supplied electricity to both Titcombe College and Egbe hospital was stolen. To date, some of these facilities have not been replaced.

11. Oladele Dada (TC No. 256) 1993-2000, another Egbe indigene, was a strict disciplinarian and an effective principal. He graduated from Ahmadu Bello University in 1963 and he was invited by popular consensus to head the institution and to restore the old glory of the College.

12. Omolade Balogun (2000 to 2006) is the third Egbe indigene to head the institution. Unfortunately, it appears that the quality of the institution has further deteriorated and is currently in the shadows of its past glories. The School appears to face challenges in funding, administration and discipline.

13. Oladele Dada (2006 to date) is the current principal of the College. He is the fourth Egbe indigene to head the institution. At the time of writing, he was still new to the institution but he too is an old student of the College. Although he shares similar names with the 11th principal, the two individuals are different.

Chapter 5: The Legacy of the Early Missionaries

There were also, of course, several non-teaching staff members whose activities complemented those of the teaching staff. Some of these people include, but are not limited to, the following: Peter Afolabi, Amos Stewart, Baba Arosanyin, Gabriel Adeyemi, Sunday Oshagbemi and Paul Balisky.

Paul Balisky came to Titcombe College in 1958. He was a hard working man and an engineer who provided and maintained the pipe borne water supply for the School. He also maintained the lighting system, the reconstruction of the auditorium, including the landscaping and construction of sports fields and workshops of the College and the Hospital. Peter Afolabi was a mechanic but he also worked with Howard Dowdell in various capacities.

Amos Stewart was a carpenter but he rose to be a manager of the workshop based at the Egbe Hospital which covered the services of both Titcombe College and Egbe Hospital. It was here that Sunday Oshagbemi, otherwise known as 'iron bar', worked in various capacities for several years before he retired. Baba Arosanyin was a carpenter and also at a point became the manager of the workshop while Gabriel Adeyemi, who hailed from Ogga, was a bricklayer. Adeyemi was in charge of the building in the College at some point during the early years. Without the efforts of some of the names mentioned above and the co-operation of the then students, the infrastructure by which Titcombe College became popular would not have existed. Above all the implicit faith and confidence in God had made all things possible.

Peter Koledade who migrated to Egbe from Ejiba was known throughout his life as a 'headmaster' because he built up Egbe Primary School to a high standard. He was awarded an OBE, a rare honour given during the Colonial era. He played the organ in the local church, was a good hunter and also a very good agriculturalist. He did not teach at Titcombe College but he had good associations with the teachers especially with Howard Dowdell. Another person who had close associations with Dowdell was David Kayode who originally came from Mopa and he was the pastor of the local ECWA Church.

The relationship which Titcombe College had with the community of Egbe was cordial. As the first class started in the local church, the influence of the community had been close in relation to Christian activities. However, like other schools in Nigeria and Africa as a whole, the College had the characteristics of isolation because of the dormitory facilities and Western stereotype cultural imitation (Brown, 1975). However, the school system cannot be isolated from the community life in which the child is expected to participate. As Egbe is predominantly a Christian community, the students participated in Sunday-School activities and Christian campaigns, i.e. evangelism. There were also the Board of Governors and the Parents/Teachers Association in which the community was adequately represented.

With almost every village now getting a secondary school, the local community has become more responsible for the College, a role the local community appears to be ill-prepared for. The danger of the College being too localised might affect the community and the activities of the old Students Association. Many members are prepared to sacrifice immensely for their alma-mater. Improvement in the school should be effected in community relationships, since local influences should be as informed as realistically as possible. Titcombe College has suffered misfortunes and the quality of its present programmes is a shadow of what it was previously. The misfortunes provide a warning that must be heeded in order to prevent the College from collapsing altogether. The entrance to the administrative building of Titcombe College is shown in Photograph 10.

Photograph 10: Titcombe College

Higher educational development

In October 2002, Bingham University was proposed as an institution to be owned and run by the Evangelical Church of West Africa. The University was named after Reverend Roland Bingham, a pioneer missionary who came to Nigeria more than a century ago. The institution obtained Federal Government's approval about two years after the proposal.

At the time of writing in 2008, preparations are underway to commence teaching in some of its faculties. The authors have reliably learnt that its faculty of science and technology will be located at Egbe, other things being equal. It is believed that the solid science foundation established at Titcombe College was one of the factors that made the policy makers of the University locate it at Egbe. At the same time, it is also believed that the solid science foundation at Titcombe College will be further enhanced if the project goes ahead as planned.

Egbe hospital – a major legacy

The history of Egbe hospital cannot be fully appreciated without paying adequate tribute to the early medical personnel and the early missionaries. Although Tommy Titcombe was not a medical doctor, he pioneered medical treatment at Egbe. He was known as 'Oyinbo Olooju' which means the white man who treats sores. Tommy was reported to go around the settlements in the bushes healing sores with packets of medicine. Sores were prevalent in the area in view of various infections obtained through muddy waters, limited modern sanitation facilities and the daily occurrence of having cuts and bites in the bushes. A dispensary was built early in Egbe after the First World War. In 1925, a new 40-bed maternity hospital was built.

In 1926 the first medical doctor, Dr Preston, arrived in Egbe and was assisted by Miss Lang, alias 'Olutoju' which means one who takes care. Later, Miss Thompson arrived and she was assisted by Mama Debora, popularly known as 'Momo Ile-ogun' which means the mother of the dispensary home. The dispensary was popularly known as 'Ayin Oro' because the buildings were behind the thorny cactus trees. It should be stated that the walls of the dispensary were built of mud and they were plastered with cement. The buildings were covered with corrugated iron sheets. The walls were maintained in a very clean condition by regularly painting them. Hundreds of children were born in these early dispensary buildings.

In 1951, George Campion and Esther Campion, both Canadians by nationality, arrived at Egbe and found that the dispensary was the best facility available for their work. George and Esther Campion performed the first Caesarean operation on a kitchen table in the house once owned by Tommy Titcombe. Marion Ross, who later became Howard Dowdell's wife, worked round the clock with Mama Deborah (Mrs Deborah Ajayi) at the dispensary where hundreds of children were delivered.

The first Hospital buildings began in 1952 and in July 1953 the buildings were dedicated. The building consisted of an operating theatre, a recovery room, a steam sterilising facility, a records department for filing permanent patient documents, a doctor's office, X-ray room and a second doctor's office.

In 1965 the following buildings were completed: pharmacy, general supply office, administrator's office, cashier's office, accountant's office and a second floor operating suite. In June 1971 the maternity building was completed and dedicated with thirty five beds and twenty six bassinettes. In 1972 there was an extension of the X-ray room and the mortuary was built and completed. Howard Dowdell helped in the operation theatre with Marion and Campion. As Campion had qualified in Canada specialising in tropical medicine he was not a qualified surgeon but he was able to perform minor and sometimes not so minor surgery.

There was a need for manpower to maintain a good water supply and electricity. Local youths were trained by Howard Dowdell to do some minor jobs in the theatre, laboratory, X-ray department and the workshop. The Nurses Training School and Midwifery School started in 1955 by Lynda Jane Kreuger, a qualified nursing teacher from the U.S.A.

Mary Wylie from Canada, though not initially a trained nurse, took care of the home for single nurses. When she went on furlough she became trained and returned as a qualified nurse. Dorothy Jackson from Canada took charge of a twenty five-bed ward. The first graduating class of five nurses was in 1959. In July 1971, the Community Nurses Training School was started with an admission of twenty girls. In 1975, the first graduating class of the Community Midwives Training School, a three and a half years programme, had seventeen passes out of eighteen. In 1976, the second graduating class, all twelve passed. The performance of the school was excellent with initially male and female admissions. Subsequently, the hospital policy was changed to accommodate only female admission.

The hospital became renowned for efficiency with the area of its services covering the whole of West Africa. When the missionaries left the hospital it was by now multi-national, multi-cultural and multi-ethnic in terms of its workforce and patients Unfortunately, since the missionaries left, the hospital has become financially impoverished. This has resulted in lower standards of service and generally poor healthcare performance. Many people wish that the missionaries had not left. It remains a challenge to the local operators even to maintain the standard of the services established by the missionaries. The entrance to Egbe hospital is shown in Photograph 11.

Readers interested in a fuller history of the hospital are recommended to read Samuel Agbo's (2002) pamphlet on the subject. The pamphlet contains separate sections on the background of and the desire for the hospital, its establishment, the problems encountered and the future challenges faced by the institution.

Photograph 11: Egbe Hospital

Christianity – another major legacy
It is obvious that the spread of Christianity was the primary purpose of the activities of the missionaries in the first place. However, in order for their converts to be able to read the Bible and follow its injunctions they had to be literate either in the English language or in their various vernaculars. Fortunately, at the beginning of the 20th Century, the Bible was being translated into many languages all over the world. This event was advantageous to the spread of the Christian religion and the growth of churches. Some people would therefore argue that,

notwithstanding its pivotal role in transforming the lives of the people, education, health-care provision and treatment were more or less secondary objectives of the missionaries. The primary objective of the founding missionaries was to convert the hitherto heathens into Christians.

Indeed, as a direct result of the teachings of the missionaries, there were several thousand converts to Christianity and the Christian ways of life. Many churches were built to accommodate several thousand new believers who were previously practising their traditional religious beliefs. Today, there are more than a dozen Evangelical Churches of West Africa (ECWA) established and functioning at Egbe. While most of the churches at Egbe are of ECWA denominations, there are a number of other denominations such as Anglican, Jehovah Witnesses, Baptists, etc. Indeed, overall, it is estimated that there are well over fifty churches operating in the town and doing well. Catholic churches have not grown in importance. Neither has the Moslem religion. However, there exists one big mosque in the town. Fortunately, there is religious harmony in the town and the current national and international Moslem versus Christian disputes do not appear to be present at Egbe. There are sometimes Moslems, Christians and traditional worshippers within the same extended family system without disruption to their social and economic activities.

Appendix 1

Hon Justice Leslie's Analysis of Egbe Problems – Extracts (1976)

In this short speech I suggest that we should all be self analytical and brutally critical of ourselves and Egbe Mekun, the cultural, political and social club of which we proudly belong. In this jet age we should stop pretending to be what we are not.

Too many of us can be bought, we are toadies and we love bickering. In intellectual capacity, we are second to none, yet this capacity is invariably misused. In my humble opinion we have been accidentally saved as an entity and town. This is not only by an incongruous attachment to churches but also by the adroitness or ingenuity of our forefathers in building a solid wall around our town to ward off aggressors during the old slave trade era. I am not arguing in the least that Egbe has not a most admirable and indeed, inventive political strength. Our religious (both native and foreign) organizations, for instance is indeed strong. However this streak is more than matched by some quite disastrous political vices.

The first of these is certain venality (corruption). There are always too many of us who can be bought, too many whose love of money and success contorts our very genuine talents. The second is self-aggrandizement or exaltation and a carefree notion, not minding what other towns and villages around us do for their own development. The result of these two weaknesses is a plethora of successful and garrulous windbags without any moral faith, which is an element fatal to political and cultural life. The third of our weakness is toadyism. This ranges from the snobbery of a sort prevalent all over Yagba land to a bowing down to factional, head's authority peculiar to Egbe alone. I attribute it to a long history of our kingmakers, starting with the erstwhile Odo-Egbe versus Oke-Egbe faction.

That some Egbe intellectuals are involved in this sort of bickering, instead of converting their energies and talents for the betterment of our people and town leaves many things to be desired. We quarrel among ourselves. When we succeed in obtaining a winning position, we fling it away. These social, political and cultural defects have so far outweighed the undoubted social and personal virtues of our people.

What should we do now? My suggestions are:

(a) Cast away old carefree attitudes to the overall development of Egbe.
(b) Vigorously involve our women-folk in this club – be they housewives or students.
(c) Invite our friends to join this club.
(d) We must make our donations free, voluntary and prompt.
(e) Barring illness, we should endeavor to attend all Egbe meetings.
(f) Adopt this attitude … "What can I do for Egbe?" And not what Egbe can do for us.
(g) Believe that there can rightly be a holy mistaken zeal in the development of our town.

These are my inclinations: to change what we can – to better what we can, but still to bear in mind that man is but a devil weakly fettered by some generous beliefs and imposition; but these should not be hindrances in our way. My hope is that we shall overcome.

Appendix 2

Messages from Reverend Tommy Titcombe to 1966 graduates of the College

Some of you will be graduating this year. May the Lord richly bless you and make you a blessing to others. The words of Paul as recorded in Acts, 9: 6, "Lord, what will thou have me to do?" have been going through my mind. How wonderful it would be if each of you on your graduation day would ask of the Lord this same question. God has a plan for each one of you and he will never ask you to do anything without giving you the necessary strength and guidance to achieve it. He will never ask you to go anywhere alone, without "I am with you always" (Matthew, 28:20).

We are all His witnesses (Hebrew, 12:1-2). What kind of witness are you going to be? Will you be a true witness for Him by laying aside the things of the world? Will you show forth the riches of His grace by the way you live? Such dedication means much to others and means peace and joy to your own lives. Remember, Jesus will never fail you.

It is now sixty-five years since I asked the Lord, "What will thou have me to do?" His answer was, "I want you in Africa, after you complete a course in Bible College." Fifty-nine years ago, I entered Yagbaland and settled in Egbe. Since that time the Lord has truly done great things for you, for which I praise Him.

The first school in Egbe was started in 1909; the first boarding school was started in August 1916. All the students were Yagba and some of these are still with you. I must say 'Good bye' and a heartily 'God bless you' and may He use each of you for His glory. Remember, 'Oyinbo Egbe' still loves you and prays for you daily.

Your old friend, Tommie Titcombe

Bibliography

Abogunrin, SO (2002), Chairman, Bingham University Implementation Committee,*Introducing Bingham University – The Proposed University of the Evangelical Church of West Africa*, Alofe (Nigerian) Enterprises, Ibadan, Nigeria.

Achebe, C (1994), *No longer at ease,* Anchor books edition, New York.

Agbo, S (2002), *History of ECWA Hospital, Egbe*, a publication made to celebrate its fifty years of service, 1952-2002, Egbe, Nigeria.

Awarun, T (1974), Oral History of Egbe, Interviews conducted by the authors.

Awarun, D (1983), Oral Traditions of Egbe, Interviews conducted by the authors.

Awe, K (1958), Interviews conducted by the authors.

Akinpelu, JA (1982), *An introduction to philosophy of education in Nigeria,* Board Publications Limited, Ibadan, Nigeria.

Aworinde, A (1974), Interviews conducted by the authors.

Awoniyi, B (1984), Egbe Chieftaincy, *Kwara Weekly Publication,* Ilorin, Nigeria.

Aworo, I (1982, 2003), Interviews conducted by the authors.

Barrow, R (1976), *Plato and Education,* Routlege and Kegan Paul, London.

Bulifant, JC (1950), *Forty Years in the African Bush,* Grand Rapids, Zondervan Publishing House.

Crowder, M (1973), *The story of Nigeria,* Faber and Faber, London.

Dowdell, HF (2002), *It Just Iappencd to Happen*, Stouffville, Ontario, Canada, Centre for World Missions, 3rd edition.

Egbe Chiefs, (1984), Representation Document.

Fafunwa, B (1980), *History of Education in Nigeria,* Allen and Urwin Limited, London.

Graham, SF (1966), *Government and Mission Education in Nigeria, 1900-1919*, Ibadan University Press, Ibadan, Nigeria.

Haney, P (1970), A speech presented at Titcombe College Assembly.

Haye, de la S (1995), *Tread Upon the Lion: The Story of Tommie Titcombe,* SIM Publishers (5th printing), Ontario, Canada.

Hiskett, M (1975), Islamic education in the traditional and state systems in Northern Nigeria, in G Brown and M Hiskett, *Conflict and harmony in tropical Africa,* George Allen and Unwin Limited, London.

Hodge, H (1934), Annual Report, No.5/1930-1934.

Hogben, T and Kirkgreen A (1966), *The Emirates of Northern Nigeria,* Oxford University Press, Oxford.

Igunnu, JB (1993), *Some Agricultural and Industrial Potentials of Egbe town in Kogi State, Nigeria,* in Bandele, S (Editor), Focus on Egbe: An Egbe Welfare Association Publication, Zaria.

Iyekolo, EB (2006), *The Peoples of Okunland,* Concept Publications Limited, Lagos, Nigeria.

Kabba Province Annual Report (1930), No.5.

Kalu, O (1978), *The Nigeria Story,* Daystar Press.

Kayode, MO (2003), A speech presented to Bishop Dr Charles Edward Blake on behalf of the Elegbe of Egbe.

Kenyo, EA, (1952), *Isedale Yoruba,* unpublished manuscript.

Kwara Weekly, (1984), September 26-29, Ilorin, Nigeria.

Law, R (1977), *The Oyo Empire, 1600-1836),* Clarendon Press, Oxford.

Leslie, SI (1976), A speech presented to Egbe people in Kano.

Nigeria Herald Newspapers (1984), September 27, Ilorin, Nigeria.

Niven, CR (1957), *History of Nigeria,* Longman, London.

Obayemi, A (1986), *Orisa – eclipsed Supreme Being: some history-graphical notes,* paper presented at University of Ilorin, April.

Ojo, GA (1966), *Yoruba Culture,* University of London Press.

Olaniyan, R (1982), *African History and Culture,* (Ed.) Longman, London.

Olokundu, I (1968), Some statements discussed with the authors.

Olorunsola, J (1970), 'Geographical description of Egbe' a paper presented at Titcombe College, Egbe.

Olu of Okeri (1984), Interview by Mark Dada (discussed with the authors).

Olumotanmi, AO (no date), *Titcombe College Egbe: A Legacy of Faith*, Olumotanmi Educational Enterprises, Minna, Nigeria.

Okun Development Association Publication (1981), 15th July.

Oshatoba, SA (1985), *SIM and ECWA in Nigeria,* Gbenle Press Limited, Ilorin, Nigeria.

Owojaiye, JA (1981), Memorandum presented to the Elegbe of Egbe.

Owojaiye, JA (no date), *Chieftaincy Institution in Egbe,* mimeograph.

Simonyan, O (1991), *Egbe Chronicle,* New Pen Publishing, Lagos, Nigeria.

Titcombe, T (1966), A letter written to Titcombe College Students.

Titcombe College, Egbe, Old Students Association (Western Zone), 1996, *'Brief History of Titcombe College',* pp. 10-12, Commemorative Brochure for the N20 million School Development Fund, Kings College Hall, Tafawa Balewa Square, Lagos, Nigeria.

Index

A
Abraham Olokundu, 41
Achebe, 98
Acknowledgements, 4
Adewumi, Job, 107
Agbo, Samuel, 113
Ainke (Ahinke, Ayinoke), 24
Ajaforunti, 17
Alafin of Oyo, 17
Alhaji SS Amego, 101
'An arranged marriage', 74
Ajetunmobi, Henry, 4, 11
Apprehentice ship system, 65
Arima publishing, 2
Asalu, Owa's deputy, 74
Awoniyi, 86
Aworo, I, 23

B
Balogun, Omolade, 108
Bayo, Oshagbemi, 4
Bingham University, 111
Brown, 110
Bulifant, JC, 39

C
Certain rights and sacrifices, 51
Chief Priest, Prophecy, 54
Chiefs held staff of office, 81
Consulting the oracle, 50
Contents, 6
Crowder, Michael, 17, 76

D
Dada, Oladele, 108
Dada, James, 1, 2, 4, 5, 13, 14
Dada, Lyndis, 15
Dale, Blummagen, 102
Dedication, 3

Deities or gods, 57
De la Haye, 13
Diane, Martin, 15
Dowdell, 13, 106
Dowry payment, 51

E
ECWA Churches, 22
Egbe general post office, 31
Egbe history and culture, 1
Egbe hospital, 23, 95
Egbe Main Market, 52
Egbe Mekun chiefs, 92
Egbe television post, 31
Elere of Ere, 40

F
Fafunwa, 53, 97
Fagbemi, Tony, 15
First Edition, 13
Foreword, 11
Frame, Charles, 106
Francis Okwudiba, 4

G
Graham, 96
Gbadeyan, Fola, 4

H
Haney, 101, 106
Harris, Poole, 102
Hiskett, 62
History of Yorubaland, 19
Hodge, H, 45
Howard Dowdell, 102

I
Idi-Obata, 74
Igbo-Ogun, 74
Igunnu, JB, 28
Indigenous religion, 56
Informal indigenous education, 63
Iyekolo, 82, 88

J
Jimoh, Akolo, 17
K
Kale, 96
Kayode, MO, 28, 40
Kelae, 17, 19, 20, 21
Kenyo, EA, 19
Kingmakers, 85
Kraakevik, 106
L
Law, R, 19
Lawiri and Ofili rivers, 23
Leslie, 117
Lord Lugard, 23
M
Missionary activities, 96
Mokobon Movement, 39
N
National Agricultural Land Development Authority (NALDA), 31
Nigerian Agricultural Cooperative Banks (NACB), 31
Niven, CR, 41
Non-teaching staff members, 109
O
Oba Aina Owojaiye, 81
Oba Joseph babalola Denki, 82
Oba James Oluremilekun Adegboyega Olokundu, 85
Oba Stanley Kayode Owa, 87
Obayemi, 69
Odo-Owon, 24
Oja-Egbe, 74
Olaoba, Babalola, 107
Olaniyan, 69
Okemesi wars, 40
Okoa, 20, 24
Okwudiba, Francis, 4
Olokundu, 80
Olu, Justus, 107
Olumotanmi, AO, 31
Oluwo hills, 17, 18

Omo Owu, 52
Opada (Ipo), 24
Oriki, praise chants, 62
Orun-Egbe, 74
Oshagbemi, Bayo, 18
Oshagbemi, Solomon, 3
Oshagbemi, Titus, 1, 2, 4, 5, 13, 14
Oshatoba, 96
Owa Oguntoshin, 20
Owa of Ilesha, 19
Owojaiye, 22

P

Preface, 13, 15
Personal rituals, 50

S

Sango, 17
Second edition, 15
Simonyan, 13, 41
Sole Administrator, 86
Sophie de la Haye, 7, 9, 80
Sudan Interior Mission, 95
Spiritual matters, 100

T

The natural name and the given name, 61
Titcombe College, 95
Title Sharers, 73
Tommy Titcombe, 13, 23, 119
Traditional African Religion, 60
Tribal marks, 59

Y

Yagba Council, 39
Yeye-Odu, David, 108